I0161926

My Love, Life

ISBN 978-0-6152-3861-6

My Love, Life

Published by
True Love Productions
A Division of Kristyn Simmons Publishing
Philadelphia, Pennsylvania

ISBN 978-0-6152-3861-6

This book is dedicated to my
ENTIRE family.

"In times of universal deceit, telling the
truth is a revolutionary act."
-George Orwell (1903-1950)

CONTENTS

Monday, December 2, 2002   Seattle, Washington

2:26am

 Hello there curious reader. This is my first zine ever and I'm really excited about making it. What is a zine? A zine- an abbreviation of the word magazine- is most commonly a small circulation, non-commercial publication of original or appropriated texts and images. More broadly, the term encompasses any self-published material of minority interest.

 Recently, my friend Deevious mentioned that he created and distributed 2 zines in his life. He told me that he included journal entries in his zines. That's when I knew that this would be my next major project.

 I'm an outgoing person who can be very anti-social. This is my way of comfortably communicating with thousands of people while still spending time alone.

<u>**THANK YOU**</u> for your support!

Wednesday, May 31, 2006   Philadelphia, Pennsylvania

6:15am

Fast forward 3 and a half years…..

Hello again! This "project" has turned into an actual book. My "first zine" is now a part of my first book. I'm quite happy about the leap. I just finished adding the last 3 and a half years onto the end of it. Although I'll be expounding upon some things mentioned in what I'd written in 2002, I'm keeping the narrative pretty much the same from when I was 26 years old. I like seeing the change in tone from one style of writing to the next. I'm sure there will be several changes before the book is complete. The point is, the bulk of it is done…. IT IS DONE!!

A full-length cd, a book, a feature length film and enough paintings for a gallery showing are all of the things that I envision doing (at the very least) before I no longer use this human body to do anything anymore. Thoughts, feelings and relationships of all sorts are primary things that fuel a sense of urgency to do what makes me happily sacrifice many hours to work on: my artistic endeavors.

For me, they are some of the greatest things that make my life worth living. They are my love or life expressed.

Speaking of my life or love…shall we begin?

Chapter 1
My Philadelphia Story

In South Philadelphia, born and raised- a playground is not where I spent most of my days. I grew up in the projects, not like the ones here in Seattle. These were real, urban projects- the ghetto. I lived there with my mother and brother until I was seven years old.

My mom could handle a lot of things: mice, cold weather, people passed out in the darkened hallways of a high-rise building we used to live in, but she could not handle flying cockroaches- the kind that don't care what you spray at them! After that episode, we moved in less than a week (so it seemed at the time) to North Philly. Its "geographical region" has changed a few times in my lifetime, so I'll be more specific. I lived between Broad and Olney and Fern Rock, which are two major public transit centers. It was nicer than the projects, but not by much.

There are a few key things that I haven't mentioned yet that I feel are important to add. My mom is African-American and Native-American. Unless you are familiar with Native-American features, you wouldn't be able to tell that it's in her genes. My father is Irish-American, I think. My mom says that he's Irish, but I'm not sure if that's true. My mom knew my father for a little more than a year and didn't ask many personal questions.

She was totally in love with him when she found out that she was pregnant. She told me (I'm not sure if she told him) that she got pregnant on purpose because she wanted a girl (my brother was 5 years old at the time). She was happy, as was my father, at first. After he went away for a weekend, things changed.

My mom suspects that a friend of his, whom she felt was racist, gave him second thoughts and made him question her intentions because my father questioned her reasons for having a baby with him and if it was really his baby. She was in her first trimester. My mom was so infuriated she told him that she didn't need him or his money and kicked him out. She dropped a picture of me off at his old place. She left it with his landlady to pass on, in case she was ever in contact with him again.

I've never seen a picture, heard his voice, nor have I received a letter to this day. I'm not sure why (perhaps because my cousin/best friend's dad had been shot when she was young), but I thought my dad was dead until I was 12 years old. I simply didn't ask my mom a lot about him because I could tell it made her uncomfortable. Besides, it wasn't strange to have fathers be absent or change in my family. I have 4 uncles and 3 aunts. They all started having kids- in and out of wedlock at relatively young ages.

My brother is 6 years older than I am. We have different fathers. His father is Puerto-Rican. He's never spoken to nor has he seen his father. My brother and I having different fathers was never a big deal to me whatsoever. I only thought about it when people asked me why we didn't look anything alike. My brother looks like a lot of the men in my family. I look like most of the women, but with a paler complexion.

It didn't even occur to me that my brother is "only" my half-brother until I was 12 or 13 years old; a classmate pointed it out. I hadn't thought about it before. It didn't change my feelings towards him in the slightest. Neither of our fathers were around and we had the same mom. We lived in the same house and shared the same family. That's all that mattered.

My brother went away to boarding school when I was 2 years old (he was 8 years old). My mom felt he'd get a better education at Milton Hershey than in the projects. My brother HATED it! (Now he's very grateful he went.) He stayed there for about 6 years. He finally came home after two runaway attempts and years of begging and pleading. At this point, I was in a private, Christian school. I wanted to attend Milton Hershey so bad (Hello?? Hershey's chocolate??? The kids who attended got to sample the new candy bars first!), but my mom wouldn't let me. She didn't like commuting there and looked forward to my brother finishing.

I was always SUPER excited when my brother came home because I would have a playmate and I loved my brother to pieces. My cousin Kyah was my playmate and best friend throughout my childhood. She protected me and openly loved me. I felt completely safe with her and loved by her, which I didn't feel oftentimes on my own.

When we moved out of the projects, we moved to a slightly better neighborhood. I didn't see Kyah nearly as much. Eventually we hardly ever saw each other at all due to distance and because my mom thought she was a bad influence on me around the onset of puberty. She was 2 years older and hung out with different crowds of people than I did. I didn't have a crowd at all.

Mom would not let me stay out past dark, even around the corner. I constantly had boys and grown men eyeing me up and down in lecherous and perverted ways, even as a child, I could feel it. In some ways, men were worse to me as a child because they figured that I didn't know any better.

I forgot to mention that I've had a very fair complexion since I was a baby. Most people think I'm Hispanic or Caucasian. My eyes are hazel and my hair was fine, dark and wavy when I was young. It became curly, as I got older. Needless to say, in predominately black neighborhoods (which was my world), I stuck out a lot, all the time.

The indoors was where I spent most of my time: at home, school or daycare. I was a latch key kid (I had a key around my neck to get into my house after school because nobody else was there). I spent PLENTY of time home alone. My uncle or neighbor would come by once in a while to check up on me, but I hardly had anyone my age play with me. Thus, when my brother was around, I was in HEAVEN!!

Then something changed when he was about 15 years old. My brother began to pull away from me. I can understand everything now in hindsight, but then, I was very confused. My brother began to hate my mom and me. He would throw things at me, yell at me and act like a real asshole. At one point, my mom was afraid to leave us alone together.

I used to think of ways I could go the rest of my life without talking to him, while living in a row home with him. For all those who don't know what a row home is, it's a home that is adjacent on both sides to other homes. My house was right in the middle of 25 houses. That's only ONE side of the street! These types of houses are all over Philadelphia. I used to think about not talking to my mom either because she would upset me so much sometimes too. My family didn't talk about problems between us. We just ignored them and each other, joked around and one day "everything would be okay again", until the next blow up. Thankfully, my mom was a passive-aggressive person, so my brother was my main adversary, which sucked because I loved him so much and only wanted to get along with him. I'm his little sister though. I'm sure I was annoying.

Home life was a stark contrast to school life. We were required to wear uniforms at school, which I loved because they were nicer than my regular clothes. My shoes were the only things that reflected my poverty. It was tough convincing my mom to buy high quality shoes instead of "payless" brands. I finally did convince her one year by promising that I wouldn't ask for another pair all year long- and I didn't. I loved those shoes too and ever since knew the satisfaction that came with investing in a good pair of comfortable, yet stylish shoes.

I DETESTED being poor. The ways my mom spent her

money drove me crazy. Mind you, she DID send me to private school, kept me and my brother fed and bought a home all on her own. I didn't appreciate any of that then. She preferred buying me more clothes (and not often) that were cheaply made, rather than the higher quality clothes that were sometimes a bit more expensive, but would last longer. My mom and I have very different tastes also. She likes frills, lace and "scenes" whereas I prefer the sleek, classic, yet SLIGHTly funky and casual.

I learned many things about life on my own because the life I was living was VERY different than any body else I knew or met. Even at school, I was enrolled in a special program that allowed me to learn at my own pace. I had to keep a certain pace, but I could go faster if I wanted. It catered to my competitive side. I wanted to keep up with the kids in my class that were at the highest levels. We learned mainly from books, not teachers. It's helped me approach learning in my adult years very similarly. I have no problem teaching myself many things from books or on my own.

My family made me laugh a lot and I knew they loved me, but after leaving the projects (where many of them lived or lived close-by), I hardly ever saw my extended family, except sometimes, at our church in those same projects, which was up the street from my grandmother's house. I attended Emanuel Lutheran church (one of the oldest Lutheran churches in Philadelphia, with German names dating back to the early 1800s) every Sunday until I was 16. It was there, like many musicians I admire, that my love of music began.

The wife of one of the pastors (they changed approx. every 5-7 years) from when I was around 10 years old used to bring in her guitar and play songs for Sunday school and during service. We've had several piano and organ players who were members of our congregation play for years. The organs that are there were all built by hand. There's a GORGEOUS one upstairs that's deteriorating due to lack of money. The sounds they made used to enchant me to no end. It's what I loved most about going to church- singing. Nobody knew that though (not even me, for a while) for I was rather shy about singing.

I always wanted to play the guitar, drums or piano, but my mom wanted me to play the flute (in third or fourth grade). That lasted for 2 years. I think that mom always wanted to play the flute and pushed me to play. I returned it one day because we got into a silly fight over it and she held it's cost over my head. I did not love it like that, so I took it back. Problem resolved. She wasn't happy about it though.

My mom worked a lot and loved television. Watching television together was our "bonding" time. My mom has never been the openly affectionate type. I think it makes her feel too vulnerable to feel comfortable expressing caring emotions aloud. She'd find other ways to show her love. My brother was a smart-ass and always said things like, "You know I hate you, right?" which to some degree, I shrugged off, but to a larger degree, sunk in. I later realized that it was his way of showing affection, for he was an adolescent male.

My family did NOT help at all when I was going through puberty. Mind you, my grandmother was dating an exotic dancer who was 20 years younger. She would crochet outfits for him and other people (including some of her children) who danced. This was no secret, yet no one talked to me about sex or even getting my period. They just assumed that I learned at some point. I did my research, but this was around 1988. The Internet was not what it is now and I attended a Christian school. I was confused (often) and sought answers wherever I could get them (thank goodness for Judy Blume!!)

By the time my brother was 16, he had developed a healthy sexual appetite. He had girls calling or coming by the house quite frequently. He also had catalogues full of sexual products, toys, videos and such that would arrive in the mail. That's where I first began to see naked people. Then, one day I found one of his porn videos. I was probably 13 or 14 at this point (my brother didn't move out until he was 23 or so). It was the first time I'd ever seen people having sex.

The two main actors were a "Catholic school girl" and her teacher. She seduced him. It was exciting to watch. It did make me aroused, but I didn't plan on having sex until I was married. I think I was around 12 years old. My hormones hadn't really kicked in yet, but I knew that sex was good and that it was best to wait until I really loved the person to do all of that with them, even though no one had ever explained that to me. I think I'd seen enough movies and heard enough love songs to know.

[This is the first time I'm telling my life story like this, so excuse me for backtracking. I'm doing my best to follow a "straight line"…]

Within a year after moving into our new house, when I was 7 years old, I was molested. My mom had this guy (a friend whom she was getting to know) over while I was asleep upstairs in my room. I had on these pajamas that zipped up from the ankle to the neck (the ones with the feet) and I remember waking up once and my zipper was halfway unzipped. Then I remembered him from earlier that night, standing at my door, saying, "Hi." I vaguely remembered him unzipping my pajamas and I distinctively remembered him licking between my legs.

At some point, I fully awoke (after he had left my room), went to the bathroom and went downstairs to be with my mom. She introduced us and I told her that we had met, that he came to my room. She said, "So that's why you had to keep going to the bathroom." She seemed like she wondered if something was up. That's all I remember. I never told my mom what happened, but I was pretty sure she knew something had happened by the way I was acting. I was sitting really close to her afterwards. We ran into that guy a few months later on the subway and I inched really close to her. I haven't seen him since. My mom and I have yet to discuss what happened, but we will soon. I know it'll be hard for her to hear and most importantly, I don't want her to blame herself.

To my mom and other parents of children who've been molested and ANY ONE who's ever been taken advantage of IN ANY WAY by any body else (and those who were around or there when it happened), please know that I don't blame anyone. We did the best we knew as who we were at that time. There's no reason to beat oneself up over abuses that we've experienced in some way, shape or form; the abuse itself is enough.

The whole incident didn't mess with my head too much because things like that - and worse- happened all the time. My mom watched the news a lot with me and I'd met other kids in my school who had been molested- some by relatives- who talked about it with me, so in a sense, I felt like it was a good thing because it helped me relate to other children in abusive situations. I didn't feel like it was my fault. I didn't feel like I was less of a person and no one has ever touched me that way- without my consent- again.

Even as a true believer in Christianity, I didn't see sex as bad. I really did my best to hold out for marriage. Many people in my Christian school felt that way, even though we had some people drop out due to pregnancy. There was no dancing allowed at the prom because they believed that dancing lead to sex, which was astonishing to me because I've danced since I could walk and didn't see myself having sex any time soon. I left that school when I completed eighth grade because my mom couldn't afford the tuition any longer.

My grades were good enough to get into the top public school in Philadelphia (Central High School). It was a 15-minute walk away from where I lived, so I was fine with the transfer. I considered attending a performing arts high school (the same school that "Boyz II Men" attended before they were "men"), but I was pretty materialistic (and afraid of performing) at the time. I thought that the pursuit of academics was the way to make money, as well as earn prestige and respect. I don't regret attending Central. It was an amazing four years. However, I still think about what it would've been like to attend a performing arts school at such a young age.

"Flashdance" was one of my favorite films at that time. I was going to be the "poor girl" with a love of dance that was going to show the judges what I could do. I had an audition set up at the school for the Creative and Performing Arts (CAPA) as a dancer, but it snowed the day I was scheduled. They set it for a later date. Before the next audition, I was accepted into Central. My fear of being judged as a dancer (it had been 7 years since I'd taken any classes) overcame me. Central was a LOT closer and it impressed people that I was accepted there, which were good enough reasons for me.

I had kissed only one boy before I started high school. He was a boy I'd met at overnight camp, at 13 years old. It was my first kiss of any kind and it was GOOD! He lived 2 hours away and his English was terrible. He was Puerto-Rican. He sent me a couple of letters and we called each other for a bit, but eventually lost touch.

My old school (the Christian one) had about 500 kids from kindergarten to twelfth grade and all of us wore uniforms. My new school had roughly 2,000 students, from ninth to twelfth grade and no uniforms. I was intimidated. I used to get busted on all the time for clothes I wore on "dress down" days at Cedar Grove Christian Academy. Now it was going to be a constant thing! I was DREADING my first day because of that fact alone. My clothes sucked!!

I ended up loving Central more than my old school. I had more freedom than I'd ever known before. My grades weren't that good, but they weren't that bad either. I was more about "working" the system because I knew how to educate myself. I made some good friends my sophomore year and by junior year, I began going to parties and drinking. I was 16 by this time. This is when I had my third kiss (my second lasted less than 2 minutes and it was terrible).

So my junior year, shortly after a very disappointing "sweet sixteen" (hardly any of my friends remembered my birthday & my mom thought that I was doing something with friends, so I did nothing.), I kissed this boy named Michael, who was biracial, like me.

His mom was white and his dad was black though. Mixed people used to always fascinate me because I hardly ever saw them. "Multi-ethnic" people weren't as common or "in" at the time (1992).

Michael was very good looking and known to be a player (someone who just "plays" the field of women- or men). I didn't care. My feelings were true and profound (in my deranged teenage/hormonal state). I didn't really know the boy and I didn't hide my feelings (from him I did, just not from me). There were FEW people that I had been strongly attracted to in my life up until then, so it all felt very serious!

I knew of his reputation and his "story". His ex-girlfriend had hurt him badly a year prior, so he wasn't looking for love (at least not YET, is what I told myself). We kissed on a few occasions throughout the year, but we were never an "item". One of the "occasions" was the night of my prom. He was one year ahead of me, so I had asked him to go with me. He just knew he was going to take my virginity that night, but I wasn't wise to his plan, or else I would've told him that there was no way I'd have sex with him any time soon.

My period started the day of my prom. He didn't believe me when I first told him. Later on in the evening, we went back to his house. His mom was away, so we had the place to ourselves. He eventually realized that I was telling the truth. As soon as he did, he got up, left me and went to his room to go to sleep. The next morning, as he drove me home, he told me that all he wanted from me was sex and that even though I seemed like a nice person; he thought it was best if we didn't see each other anymore. I was a little hurt, but I was happy that he was at least honest with me. He was also leaving/graduating in a month and I didn't have to see him around school much longer, which made it all a lot easier.

By this time (end of my junior year), I had a core group of friends that I hung out with inside and outside of school. I didn't consider myself a Christian anymore. After studying Greek mythology, I couldn't take it seriously as "the one true religion"; knowing that the Greek people felt the same way about a religion we now look at as "mythology". It changed my perspective forever. High school was the first time I examined and learned about different religions without any sort of bias. The world began to look completely different to me- more wondrous and exciting than what I had grown accustomed to seeing.

My mom worked graveyard shifts, so I had the house to myself almost every night since my sophomore year. My brother wasn't home often and he lived in the basement, with his own entrance. Friends would come over and stay the night since there was no one there to tell us what to do. We'd talk, watch cable, and occasionally drink until 3am or 4am. We stayed out of trouble and enjoyed our freedoms.

I had the life! Even though my grades were just okay, I assumed I'd get into college, like most of the other people who graduated from my school. I always tried to be studious, but I continuously got caught up in the emotional lives of my friends, to the detriment of my studies. Every time I questioned helping a friend in emotional need or meeting the demands of my workload, my friends' needs generally won. Unfortunately for my scholastic advancement, I had many friends with emotional needs at that age.

Looking back, I see that I was compensating for a lack of open love and sincerity at home. I greatly enjoyed people's emotional dependence on me. It felt good to be there for others because I felt I had few people to turn to and longed so badly for openly loving and caring affection with other people (I wasn't conscious of this at the time). My journal was always my "rock".

A friend in Cedar Grove had given me my first diary for my thirteenth birthday. I haven't stopped writing in one since. I knew that having some kind of outlet to process emotions was very important. Journals allowed me to go on and on and on about whatever boy I liked or whatever I was pissed off about or any dreams I cared to envision. They were my "safe place". It took some time (3 or 4 years) before I got over the fear of others reading them. It's interesting to read them and see how long it took for me to become honest with myself-inwardly and outwardly. Keeping a journal helped a lot in that regard. I had a few friends during those times talk to me about suicide and had known of people who'd gone through with it. People's feelings, as well as my own, have played a major role in my life. Journaling helps me to keep them balanced.

One of my closest friends had an alcoholic father who used to beat her. She was small and skinny too! Her parents were straight from Russia. She said that was just how it was (for her, not all Russians). I wished so badly that I could do something to stop it from happening, but all I could do was be there for my friend as a friend, however she needed me to be. Two of my other friends ran away from home and stayed at my house for a few days at separate times. The rest of my friends just liked getting away from their homes and chillin' at my house, since my mom would pretty much leave us alone. A common remark I'd hear was, "Your mom's house is so homey, so comfortable."

My mom didn't like me having friends over all the time. It was usually only one at a time and mainly on the weekends, but almost EVERY weekend. I LOVED it! It was the first time I felt like I was truly connecting with people. I loved being a haven for those who felt like they had nowhere to go for oftentimes I had felt that way myself. I used to wish that I had some place to go where I felt completely loved and like I belonged.

My friends helped me create that environment in my own home. They gave me a sense of pride in my home and neighborhood that I'd never known before. The funny thing is, I used to be ashamed of where I lived because it wasn't a "good neighborhood", compared to where many of my friends lived, but they loved being at my house, which made me feel good (accepted). They made me appreciate my life in countless new ways and they didn't even realize it. It's one of the reasons I had no problem giving as much as I did as a friend. I was grateful to have friends- period.

Most of my friends were white. As I mentioned earlier, my neighborhood was predominantly black. Many of my friends were raised in multiracial communities/neighborhoods. In ways, some of my friends were more "black" than I was, in terms of cultural stereotypes. I didn't like being half black and half white. For a while, during my pubescent years, I wanted to just be one or the other. Then I wanted to be just white for a year or so. I especially did NOT like being poor. Even though my family is black doesn't mean that they weren't prejudiced against black people. They had something racist or stereotypical to say about EVERYBODY! It was part of their sense of humor.

I was raised not to trust black people. I'd hear some of my family members in the projects say things like, "Goddamn black people ain't no good!" and curse their own race, but didn't want anyone else to do the same. It was very odd, but that's the way it was. They didn't trust white people either, for different reasons. Many people, in poor communities, don't trust any body, sometimes, not even themselves, yet another reason I detested poverty so much. I now see that the same distrust runs in wealthy and affluent communities as well.

My family, for the most part saw white people (in church, on TV, at work) as well mannered and financially well off with more opportunities in the world and thus, naturally happier. I saw where they came from and agreed on many points. I had never had close, white friends- aside from camp friends (far away) and a couple from Cedar

Grove who had abnormal lives (one ran away to my house and the other was Mennonite). So having all of these white people in my life and over my house was not a small thing. No one ever gave us any trouble. We might have caused trouble for some of my neighbors at times. It frequently surprised me how comfortable my friends were in my neighborhood and in my house.

My friends embraced black culture more than I had and ended up teaching me a lot about rap and hip-hop, among other things that I'd deviated from around sixth and seventh grade with the onset of heavy metal and a love of MTV during the Adam Curry (Headbanger's Ball) days, which was fostered by my mom! She loved Guns 'n' Roses (While I was still in Christian school, my mom had a big ol' crush on Axl Rose.), Skid Row, Poison and even took me to a Bon Jovi concert where we had a blast!!

Roxanne Shante and Slick Rick were the last rappers I remembered hearing regularly. I grew up listening to "black radio stations", but again, that all changed with my newfound love of heavy metal (not death metal). My brother was a HUGE Prince fan, but he's in a category all to himself. So when my friends were playing The Roots, The Beatnuts, MC Lyte, Beastie Boys, The Alkoholics, Queen Latifah, A Tribe Called Quest, Monie Love, The Pharcyde, and Cypress Hill, I was lost, at first. I liked Cypress Hill the most because they rapped a lot (in ways that were fun and fairly easy to learn) about smoking weed and drinking malt liquor, which my friends and I did OFTEN!

I loved to sing more than rap. I watched a lot of music videos (we got cable in 1988. MTV and I grew up together) and gravitated to the big names. I grew up listening to Motown, oldies (Jackie Wilson, Aretha Franklin, Marvin Gaye, Diana Ross), disco and "love songs" on the radio, as I fell asleep. I was generally open to whatever moved me, regardless of whether it was seen as "white music" or "black music".

I think some of my friends seriously wished they were black because they got so much shit for being white and genuinely loving the things they loved, such as: hip-hop (before it was a common term), rap, smoking blunts, drinking 40's and dressing in an "urban, hip-hop" style (1993 "grunge" era). I enjoyed all of those things too, but not to the same degree or with the same enthusiasm. I was more into Madonna, Prince, Michael Jackson, George Michael and Janet Jackson, basically, pop music. I loved dancing, singing, writing and spending time on the phone as well as in person with friends.

Jeans and tee shirts are what I wore most of the time, with Doc Martens (given to me by friends when they were done with them because I couldn't afford them). I'd gotten over my clothing/material obsession by my junior year. Theresa was the only friend I'd kept in touch with from Cedar Grove (one who ran away to my house). Borrowing her clothes is what helped get me through my first 2 years at Central. I loved her so much for allowing me to do that and never having issues with me about it. Some times I borrowed from other friends and it became a big issue. I became selective about whom I'd ask things from and only borrowed from those I trusted and who trusted me.

At the end of my junior year (16 years old), I became friends with this boy named Patrick. We first met on a ski trip (annual event that a bunch of kids from school did on their own) the previous winter. He got so sick one night, lost his toothbrush, and asked to use mine the next morning. Disgusting, I know, but he was a friend to other guys I knew well. He was cool and funny and asked very nicely, so I agreed, as long as he promised to wash it out REALLY well in scalding hot water for a few minutes (yes, it's a very strange way to be introduced to someone). I'm not even sure how we started talking a few months later, but we became best friends. He had a girlfriend that he was attempting to lose his virginity with (she was a virgin too) and I was helping him out as much as I could.

He made me laugh so much. He was the first guy I ever felt COMPLETELY comfortable with whenever we talked or spent time together. It wasn't until one of my best girl friends started probing me about him that I realized how much my feelings for him had grown and that they had become romantic. Afterwards, she was relentless!! She would sing, "I can't fight this feeling anymore" (by REO Speedwagon) during class, over the phone, walking down the street and would constantly threaten to tell Patrick how I felt if I didn't. I swore I'd never tell her anything I wanted to keep a secret again.

I didn't feel ready to tell Patrick anything and I didn't like being pressured about it (at all), but I did feel like it was inevitable at that point. The few times I had really liked a boy romantically (from afar), I had just kept my mouth shut about my feelings towards them. I had kissed a few guys since Michael, but nothing lasting or serious. I was VERY nervous about my romantic feelings towards Patrick for they were totally unfamiliar to me, but I was naturally comfortable with him. I didn't care if anything romantic ever happened between us. I was glad just to have him in my life.

That year I was invited to the senior prom by a boy named Jay. He was best friends with another senior boy named Devon whom I felt was "too sexy". I had the phrase written on my book bag in honor of him. Devon had a girlfriend and was about to leave for the Navy after graduation. I used to visit the library, where he'd oftentimes do work/study or hang out. He was really smart, sexy and FINE! Even though I knew I wasn't going to get with Devon any time soon, if ever, I didn't feel right even kissing Jay after the prom due to the feelings I had for Devon for the past year or so. The prom was a lot of fun. I danced all night. Once we got back to Jay's place though, I went right to sleep.

Devon and I had a history that went back a few years. We met on New Year's Eve of 1990. One of the first friends I'd made at Central invited me to her house for New Year's Eve. She invited Devon over too and we brought in the New Year drinking sparkling cider. He thought that it was champagne at first and refused. I found that very admirable, considering his age and how many would've been disappointed by the cider! He took interest in me and showed it in school.

One day, someone asked me if he was gay (he had shoulder-length hair and a pretty face). I was mortified that someone thought I was hanging out with a boy who looked gay. I was starving for other people's approval still and pushed Devon away because of it. I really liked him too, but that was that. He got a girlfriend and I moved on….then I came back. For Devon was athletically built and smart with an intensity and sensuality that oozed from his pores. A close friend, Kate, and I used to write erotic stories back and forth to each other about him. He was "unattainable" to us. I didn't take my lust for him seriously even though the feelings were very serious!

On June 13, 1993, I was on the phone with Patrick, helping him get his life in order, when I said, "So what do you want Patrick? What do you REALLY want??" I had asked him that question several times over the previous weeks and I always wanted him to say that he wanted me, but he'd always say something else. That night, my heart beating hard and fast, he finally said it.

When the word/answer, "You." came out of his mouth, I nearly died!! I was speechless (which is a rare occurrence for me, still). I had only briefly kissed maybe 6 boys up until then. I hadn't gone further than being felt up a couple of times by Michael. I was 16 and a half and about to have my first boyfriend. It seemed so unreal and perfectly natural, yet I was scared and excited at the same time for I'd seen so many romances end in pain. I wasn't sure if I was ready to take such a risk with my heart. I loved this boy more than life itself though and my hormones were on fire for him (due to my love for him, not lust for I didn't think he was that cute.).

The next day we saw each other and it was all over. He came back to my house after school and we passionately kissed, like there was no tomorrow, for over an hour- from the living room, to the kitchen and back. Yes, all we did was kiss- neck included- but it was all so intense and amazing, for I'd never cared so much for someone I'd kissed before, nor was I ever anyone's girlfriend while kissing them. He had to leave to go home, which was tough. Being with and kissing Patrick was better than anyone I had been with, by far. It was weird to think of us as "officially" together, but I liked getting used to it.

I had my first job as a counter girl at a pizza place that summer in Kate's neighborhood, Mt. Airy, where I hung out half the time. It was about a 20-minute bus ride away from my house and was the first ethnically diverse neighborhood I'd ever experienced. That summer, I had my first cigarette with Kate. I used to smoke on the weekends with her. I stayed at her house often. Mt. Airy was where a couple of my closest friends lived and hung out. That year, I experienced many "firsts". That summer marked some major changes. I was with my first boyfriend (many "firsts" there), I started listening to and loving Jane's Addiction (rebellious, yet enlightening music) and I was about to be a senior.

During that previous spring, one day after school, one of my best friends named Cindy (always got straight A's) suggested that we buy a $10 bag of weed, take it back to her house and smoke it. I had already smoked a joint at a party she threw not long before that while her parents were away. Juliet was at the party and was comfortable with it. I trusted her, so I did it, but I got really sick because I was drunk. Cindy and I were curious how we'd feel with just weed (marijuana). We each rolled a joint burrito-style (rolled it up on the table like it was a burrito), went to a nearby cemetery and got so stoned as we questioned whether or not we were really stoned. Once we made it to the 7-11 (walking), we knew. I barely smoked weed after that, not until the next year.

Virgins all around me were dropping like flies, to the point where it seemed abnormal not to have had sex, which seemed to happen rather quickly! I was curious about sex, but I knew it would be painful (I'm not a fan of pain), at least at first and I simply wasn't sure if Patrick and I were ready to go there yet. Patrick and I clicked incredibly well physically. We had terrific chemistry. Even though he wasn't the best-looking guy I'd been attracted to, he was cute, funny, obviously cared for me a lot and was honest- as was I. We'd just look at each other and be severely turned on, however, I simply didn't want to do too much, too soon.

Two and a half months into our relationship, I began considering the real possibility of us having sex. I started to feel ready and thought he was the perfect person to have sex with. Patrick was away on a camping trip with his friends when I decided that I was going to go through with it. I had no reason to doubt where Patrick was or what he was doing, but I had this weird dream one night, while I was feverishly sick (just for 2 days), that stood out to me during the week he was gone.

In the dream, my grandmother's boyfriend had raped me. It was so bizarre that I looked up a possible interpretation in this dream book my mom had, and it said, "a loved one will betray you with another". I had bought Patrick a pair of sneakers for his birthday 2 weeks prior. My mom told me beforehand, "Never buy a man sneakers. It means he's going to walk out on you." That didn't apply to Patrick though. I knew without a doubt how much he loved and adored me. I had never felt so secure in someone's love for me who wasn't family.

He told me that he would return from his trip on Friday night or Saturday afternoon. I called him on a whim Saturday afternoon, just to see if he was back yet. He answered the phone. He said that his family was in the middle of a barbeque and he asked if he could call me back. I said something nonchalantly, hung up the phone and went into the basement, where my brother was living (he wasn't there, but his kick-ass stereo was). I put on "Black" (very sad and emotional song) by Pearl Jam and cried my heart and soul out for the first time ever. I knew that it was over; that what we had was gone. In an instant, my whole world faded to black and there was nothing I could do to bring it back.

Patrick called me later on and explained that he didn't go to the shore with his friends, but instead went to visit this girl whom he had known since kindergarten. He had mentioned her before and I was never jealous. He gave me no reason to be. No one's me and I cannot be anyone else and we loved each other. That's all that mattered to me. I was more prone to being jealous of people's material advantages than "other women". At times I'd been very jealous of other girls' bodies, but

I refused to think low of myself due to some guys' horniness, as far as jealousy was concerned. I knew then that I was a unique individual with a heart that many wished they could feel love from. Love was one of the most important things to me then too, just on a smaller scale.

They didn't have sex while Patrick was visiting, but the girl came back with him. A good friend of his told me (Patrick had stopped calling me after our first conversation while this girl was in town) that he'd bet his house that they'd have sex before she left (after one week). I found out how and why our relationship was over from his friends. He wouldn't return any of my phone calls. I could hardly believe what a coward he was.

That's when I became a full-time smoker. I went from feeling hurt to angry to numb. I could not believe that he had treated me that way and that I was in love with a guy who would treat me that way. I didn't see it coming, which was the toughest part of all. I wished that he had the strength not to get with someone else in the first place, but even so, I wished he had the courage to tell me right away and to tell me himself. Who was this boyfriend of mine that I chose to give the precious gift of my whole heart? He was a horny, teenage jerk and imbecile is who he was (to me then).

My friends were all terrific. They helped me a lot!! They were really there for me. They showed me a non-blood, yet familial love that I'd never experienced before. One of the hardest parts was the fact that I still loved Patrick very much and we were about to start school, senior year, and my heart was in "intensive care". I finally talked to Patrick a week before school began (I refused to return his phone calls when HE was ready to talk). He told me that the girl, Tammy, might be pregnant and if she was, he wanted to keep the baby. Talk about a slap in the face! Why was I in love with this boy? Why him??

Thank goodness Tammy wasn't pregnant. I was still "in love" and somehow (I plead- love sickness and teenage hormones) Patrick and I ended up making out in the hallways around school here and there after a month or so went by. We had an on again, off again romance all throughout that school year. I knew that I only wanted to be with him (he knew this too), but he couldn't resist all the booty being thrown his way, since he and his friends became "super cool" that year. The ironic thing is, he and his friends used to make fun of the "cool guys" during their years at Central. They became exactly what they despised, but it was "okay", because it was now their turn to be "the popular guys".

Patrick kissed two of my best friends that year. The first one, he actually dated for a couple of months. She, Paula, grew up with Kate. We had hung out in Mt. Airy together a few times, but her mom was a lot stricter than my mom or Kate's mom. Even though he thought it was a very strange relationship (not nearly the love and passion we had), Paula was a very beautiful girl- very exotic looking and petite, with an awesome sense of style. She and Patrick shared a love of rap and hip-hop, which I didn't have at the time.

Paula had asked me if I as okay with her dating Patrick. The fact that she wanted to already felt like a small betrayal. In ways they seemed better suited though. I tried not to care that they had hung out a couple of times, but I did. I lost my virginity to Patrick at his friends' house after a Halloween party (I wasn't drunk, just dumb and in love). I didn't know when I'd feel that strongly about a person again.

I felt ready to have sex and Patrick felt like the right person to explore that realm with for I didn't want to wait to fall in love with someone else before having sex (casual sex was not an option). It was about a week or two before he and Paula started going out, "officially". Don't use reason to figure things out here. We had sex for one night every 2-3 months that whole year, until finally, I said, "No more". I couldn't deal with his mood swings anymore. I demanded all or nothing.

Just then, Devon came back into town, fresh out of the Navy. It was the summer after my graduation. I was happy to have made it through high school and into college (Penn State University). The lust I felt towards Devon my last two years at Central was still there. He was just TOO SEXY for his own good! He was 2 years older than me and so comfortable with himself (but not in a vain way) that I was a little intimidated by him. He used to flirt with me in high school, but I didn't think he really wanted to be with me.

I forgot to mention that I almost cheated on Patrick with Devon the previous summer. I ran into Devon, while with a friend, right before he was about to leave for the Navy. He asked me to chill with him, which shocked me, for we hadn't hung out outside of school since the prom; before that was the time at my friend's house in ninth grade. I didn't know if we'd ever hang out again.

We were talking in his room at his house and at some point, he touched my stomach (fairly low and I do not recall why), for a second, but nothing more. It made me nervous though. I was so attracted to him that just being in the room with him felt like I was cheating on Patrick, however, I knew that I would never cheat. I really wanted to spend some time with Devon before he left and I'm very glad that I did. I'm also glad that nothing happened, then.

One year later, Patrick was being an ass, once again, and I'd grown tired of his antics and attitude. Devon had returned from the Navy, in August of 1994, for good. We ran into each other unexpectedly and happily on South Street (a popular commercial area). I saw him right when he was about to pass me and I remembered how much he hated cigarettes, so I instinctively threw the cigarette that I was smoking away and hid my habit from him.

By the end of our second date, which began watching "The Lover" at his house, in his room, while his mom was away for the weekend, we were going at it like rabbits! It was insane!! Years of pent up sexuality came GUSHING out- repeatedly! We were a sexual match made in heaven. I wore the biggest smiles during those days!

Devon was a phenomenal lover and I was a very willing participant. We were together for almost a year, but his jealously and possessiveness drove me away. He didn't like the amount of time I spent with my friends. I was in school and working part-time, which took up a lot of my time. He didn't like many of my friends. I didn't care for his condescending attitude and he had some anger issues to work out as well. I finally broke up with him in June of '95, but it was over for me months prior. It was a bitter break up.

I loved Devon with all of my heart. We weren't healthy for each other though. He had plans to move to North Carolina in August to live with his dad and attend school there. It was a cheaper and easier life for him there than in Philly. I tried to wait to break up with him right before he left, but it became too hard to wait. We were fighting incessantly. We had very satisfying "break-up sex", 2 weeks before he left Philly. It was a tough battle for his friendship over the next 4 years.

Towards the end of my senior year (1994) I became friends with these extremely handsome twin boys. The first time I met them, I was tripping on a microdot (mescaline- a hallucinogenic). We all immediately loved each other (beyond the drug induced state). The twins, Jim and Tim, had serious problems with drugs and alcohol (crazy childhood) since puberty, but they had great, big hearts, they were funny, sang all the time and were nice and sweet guys. I loved them and they loved me and that's all that mattered.

They both had girlfriends too, so I felt relaxed around both of them without sexual tension. I knew I'd never initiate anything sexual with either of them. At some point I was attracted to Jim, but I fell in love with Tim (before and after Devon). I didn't care if I was ever sexually involved with either of them ever in my lifetime. Being around them was so much fun! In September of '95 (shortly after Devon moved), I moved into my first apartment in west Philly with the twins.

It was a HUMONGOUS place! It was the first time any of us (in our group of friends) had lived on our own. We each had our own big room for only $200. The rent was RIDICULOUSLY low for this gorgeous place right next to Drexel's campus , which borders the University of Pennsylvania's campus. In October, Paula moved into my room because she loved our place, wanted to move out of her mom's and liked that it was conveniently located and within walking distance to center city. My room was big enough for the both of us and allowed us to pay only $100 per month a piece…those were the days.

Due to our drinking, drugs (for me, marijuana and hallucinogens) and nicotine habits (all of us smoked cigarettes), we constantly scrounged for money. Being next to Drexel and walking distance from UPenn (Ivy League), two schools with very rich students that like to party, the twins were in alcoholic heaven. Whenever we had nothing, there was always a party they could easily crash not far away. I didn't care much for meeting strangers or parties. I preferred to stay at home chillin' with my friends watching movies, listening to music and/or talking.

They would've gone to more parties, but by that time, Jim had "come out of the closet". I had no idea he was gay, but it didn't make me think of him less or love him differently. Tim was figuring out who he was. That's from my point of view, not his. He now says that he always knew that he was gay. The twins were usually nervous that someone would find out that they were gay (Tim had dated a boy by this time and Jim had a boyfriend) at one of the parties and ridicule or hurt them because of it, therefore the campus parties were reserved more for times of bravery or desperation.

Being high on herb was my favorite altered state. I tripped on LSD several times while living there, but I never looked for it. I usually had it because the twins had come across it, brought it home and asked me to trip with them. I didn't trust manmade acid as opposed to something natural, such as psilocybin/mushrooms. The latter were my favorite, but much harder to come by. I was at Penn State University's Abington campus full-time and working part-time with Paula.

By the end of November (19 years old), I was head over heels in love with Tim. He had dated a guy for about a month when we first moved into the new pad, but hadn't "declared" himself gay yet. He says now that he never said that he was bisexual, but I know that he did. He seemed like he was sorting his sexuality out as many from high school were. Tim resented that Jim was pretty much kicking him out of the closet as opposed to coming out in his own way on his own time. I figured he was gay, but I didn't care one way or the other. I loved him to pieces and I still had the strong urge to kiss him.

One night, around Thanksgiving, we were really drunk (a frequent occurrence) and Tim kissed me. I was so flattered and smitten with the littlest physical affections that he showed me, for it was like a dream come true. We kissed on a few occasions afterwards. Our relationship didn't change that much. We were already best friends that lived together and sometimes we slept in the same bed together. We did have sex a few times, but not on a regular basis. I wasn't sure what I wanted from Tim. I hadn't given it much thought. I enjoyed what we had for what it was.

Did I mention that Jim and Tim were alcoholics?? They fought a lot (understatement)!! Our apartment had become "the party place". Since we were the first of all of our friends to have our own place- and we had a big ass crib- our friends were constantly at our place, bringing 40s (40 ounce bottles of malt liquor) and food, as well as weed and movies. It would be a bit much at times, with the 4 of us living together, work and school. It was freeing and awesome at first, but it began to get old after 4 or 5 months. I'd grown tired of the constant drama of the life I had going on all around me

I had finally come to terms that Tim ideally wanted me in a man's body, so the first big change I made was to stop being sexually involved with Tim. Those times in that apartment, I often describe as some of the best of times and the worst of times. Tim gave me HELL for about a month when I broke things off with him. It was awful. I swore then that I wouldn't live with someone with whom I was romantically involved. It was worse because he was one of my best friends. Things between us eventually settled down. I had sex with him one last time, (about 2 months later, the beginning of spring) when he wasn't drunk (which was a first for us) because he really wanted to and it was very sweet. I'm grateful for that memory.

In January or February of '96, I began working at a smoke shop close by our house. It was basically the only one in all of Philly and was well known among smokers- of all sorts. I had been there for about a month when I met the "Motorcycle Man". He used to come in to buy clove cigarettes all the time. I used to pray that I'd be there for the 3 minutes that he was in the store. I would die when I saw him because he was so FINE, to me.

One day, he caught me staring at him, blatantly, from the store window after he left. Of course it was the day I was sick and disgusting with a big ol' sweater on! I was mortified!! However, a few hours later, he called the store and asked me out on a date. Yeah, I was shocked, stunned and beside myself.

I found out that Mack was his name and he was 26 years old with long, curly brown hair (which I was never into, but it suited him well) that he wore in a ponytail or braided and he had bright, green eyes. I was 19 years old. I was intimidated by him because of his age, his intelligence, his looks, and his success (he was independently wealthy). He was a tele-funding manager for the Philadelphia Art Museum. He had saved a lot of money with them and other organizations over the years. No one I knew had ever done anything like that.

Courtesy of the public library system, Mack was extremely book smart. He inspired me to read for pleasure, something I hadn't done for many, many years (and even then, it was seldom). Sometimes we just hung out and read, while lying on the couch at opposite ends, rubbing each other's legs. I loved being able to ask him many questions about various subjects at any time. It was so nice to have him next to me while we read. It was all quite different from the life I'd been leading up until then.

We met in April ('96). Mack told me that at the end of May, he was going on a road trip across the country on his BMW motorcycle and that he was going to settle in Olympia, WA. I had plans to move to Seattle in September of that year. One of my best friends from high school, Juliet, had moved out there and loved it. I told him that we planned to get a place together (I'd decided this when she came to visit sometime that year.). Olympia's only 30 minutes from Seattle, so it was perfect! I wasn't sad about him leaving because I knew I'd see him again.

Our relationship was strange though. We weren't mushy with each other- at all. We wouldn't talk about our feelings for one another, which I didn't like, but didn't want to push. I was also still thinking (and feeling) a lot about Tim. Mack and Tim were as different as night and day! It wasn't fair to compare them, but I did. I craved more emotionally from Mack, more of a connection, like what I had with Tim. Tim was jealous of Mack too. Mack came over to my place from time to time, but we spent most of our time at his place because he lived alone. We had more privacy- and peace, which I began to steadily crave.

The summer of '96 was my last summer living on my own in Philadelphia. Our apartment went from good to bad to worse by June. We didn't have heat or hot water (for the dryer or shower) for the last 2 months we were there because we hadn't paid the gas bill all year. Someone broke in (while Paula was in the house. She didn't know until after they left.) and took our small television. Paula was scared shitless- and none of us knew, because we were all staying at other people's places by then.

Due to my friend Leah (whom I met through the twins and Kate), I had a job working as a Girl Scout camp counselor that summer. I had been working there for a little more than 2 weeks, when I met Maxine. I still recall first meeting her. She was a warm, tropical breeze that entered the living room one afternoon while I was at my friend Bill's house, where I was often that summer.

She was a friend of Dick's, who was a friend of Bill's. Dick is also Paula's ex-boyfriend. Dick was our extra roommate who didn't pay rent. Maxine blew me away immediately. She was just as intoxicated by me as I was by her (I didn't know this at the time). Her energy was astounding. She's half Latina and half black and positively BEAUTY full! Both of us really come alive in the summer (so we learned). It's "our season".

The same day we met, Bill (one of my best friend's from Central, with whom I smoked weed and had endless, philosophical conversations) had a party, for his parents were in Europe for 3 weeks and we all got WASTED! Five of us (3 girls and 2 boys) moved the party upstairs after most people went home or were passed out. Someone put on Bob Marley's "Coming in from the Cold" and we began to give each other massages- all of us- on Bill's parents' bed. I was massaging Maxine when she turned around and kissed me.

I had kissed a couple of girls before (as a kid, for "practice"; and as a teen, once, with Juliet, out of sheer curiosity), but none compared to this. Bill, Dick and this girl named Gia (went to Central too) were there. I kissed Gia too, which was awesome! I felt more emotionally drawn towards Maxine, though Gia was gorgeous. Bill and Dick wanted to somehow be involved with me, but I wasn't interested in either of them sexually, not even to kiss (I didn't care for Dick as a person and Bill was a good friend). I didn't know either of the girls, so it was easier to express myself sexually with them in that state during that time. Somehow I ended up just being with Maxine and I was perfectly content with her all night long.

I don't recall much, after a point, but I woke up happy in a hammock on the porch, the next morning. I was supposed to go to work at camp that day. I never went back. I missed my troupe, but I knew I was leaving for Seattle soon. (I had a thing about "good-byes" and confrontation). There was no weirdness between Maxine and I, just a few questions, which we were comfortable asking. It was all good. I wasn't exactly sure how she felt towards me, but I was okay with whatever since I was leaving in less than 2 months and Maxine was going back to school in the Midwest (she attended a well known music conservatory because of her voice) around the same time.

Maxine is a woman of many talents. I knew that I had talents, but I had no idea what they were. I'd never heard Maxine sing, but I knew that she could sing opera and that she got into a top-notch music school for training. She had a very busy schedule, so I didn't see her often. Every time we did see each other, we had this chemistry between us. We kissed once more after that night (of the party) before she left Philadelphia. She was processing a painful break up where she found out that her first boyfriend had cheated on her (I knew the feeling all too well). I wasn't sure if I'd ever hear from her again. We promised we'd write, but what did that mean?

She had had sex with Bill and Dick throughout that summer too. No lines were drawn or labels formed between any of us. I had my eyes on Mack who was now in Olympia. Maxine and Gia were the only people I had kissed since I'd kissed him. I wasn't concerned about "where things stood" romantically with Maxine. I was enamored with her, but I had no expectations of our relationship. However, it was then that I knew that I could have strong feelings for a woman and still feel no less towards men and I soon realized that I had no idea what I REALLY wanted from either of them.

Throughout this time ("summer of love"- Bill's catch phrase for that period), I distanced myself from a lot of my friends. I got my first taste of Zen Buddhism from Bill's dad. He gave me a copy of Suzuki's "Zen Mind, Beginner's mind"- changed my life forever. I was shoplifting (Banana Republic), and drug trafficking (herb), all while experiencing life for the first time in one of the richest and oldest neighborhoods in Philadelphia- Chestnut Hill (the neighborhood right next to Mt. Airy). It had so many trees, parks and cute shops. I wished that his home was my home.

For instilling the love of reading in me, I am forever grateful to Mack. Gloria Naylor's "Mama Day" is a book of his that he gave to me to read while with him one day. I ate it up! From there, I began exploring the library, for the first time looking at books that really interested me apart from school assignments. Around this time, a friend recommended Alan Watts as an author that I would enjoy. The first book he suggested that I read was, "The Book: On the taboo against knowing who you are."

Alan Watts helped me to better understand Zen Buddhism. I fell in love with his writings. Over the years, I read all of his books. It was while reading "Nature, Man and Woman" (in Seattle) that I clearly saw the image of a snake on my back as a tattoo. Alan Watts felt like more of a friend to me than many I was closest to (thus began the distance from many of my friends), which is why I read his words carefully and watched all the videos that I found on him. He made me literally laugh out loud. My brain was titillated, my spirit expanded and I breathed more harmoniously due to his influence over the years.

I ended up living at Bill's house for a little bit shortly before I moved. I loved his parents, their house, the neighborhood and they traveled a lot that summer. Bill was leaving soon for college too, so it was nice to spend what time I could with him. I was selling nickel and dime bags so I could smoke weed for free. I got a personal loan from my bank for $5,000 to take care of some credit card debt and to have some "extra cash" for my move to Seattle.

The end of August was quickly approaching. I was all set to leave. I loved my friends immensely, but I didn't feel like confronting their sadness over my departure. I was excited at the prospect of living in a new and beautiful city. I was happy and wanted to remain that way, at least until after I left. So without any goodbyes to just about all of my closest friends, I left for Seattle, Washington. My relationship with almost all of them hasn't been the same since.

Chapter 2
The Emerald City

Before I moved to Seattle, I knew I was going to love it. Juliet told me all about Seattle's natural beauty (thus the reason it's called "The Emerald City"- all of the GREEN). We both have a true love for Nature. We became friends as a result of this connection. It was our love of Jane's Addiction that brought us together (they are all about the love of Mother Nature). The natural environment was a BIG incentive for my move. I was tired of the tons of concrete all around me. I had no clue what I was in store for.

As soon as I arrived at the airport, I could smell the difference in the air. It was so fresh, clean and crisp. It was a little colder than I had expected, but that was fine by me. I was out of Philadelphia! It was the first time I'd ever left the east coast. It was also my first flight (l like flying). We headed straight for Juliet's place. She lived in a boarding house in the University District- University of Washington area. I stayed in her room, with her awesome kitten named Zo-Zo, for one month.

In the beginning of September (a few days after I arrived), Juliet gave her notice to vacate the premises by the end of the month. She was working three jobs, so it was pretty much up to me to find a place for us. I love doing that kind of stuff, looking through classifieds and bulletin boards, but I had no idea where all the different streets were, in and around Seattle. Using maps helped, but it was still a bit of a challenge.

Time was quickly running out. It was Friday, we had to move by Monday and we had no place to go (for us, yes, but not all of our stuff) if we didn't find a place. Juliet was severely stressed out about this, but for some reason, I felt like something would work out. I scheduled an appointment to look at a place in Capitol Hill (one of 3 cool- and convenient- neighborhoods that we narrowed our search to) on Saturday or Sunday afternoon. It was a 2-bedroom apartment, a half block from a 24-hour supermarket, a library, and a small shopping mall. It was 2 small blocks from a major street. It had a fireplace in the large living room and 2 sinks in the bathroom- for only $650/mo.

The apartment gods were smiling down upon us, but we didn't have the place yet. We submitted our applications right away. Juliet was freaking out because she had a lot to move (she had 3 jobs, remember?) and we had to deal with all of the paperwork to apply to this place the same weekend that we had to pack. We got the call on Sunday (or

Monday morning) saying that it was ours. I still don't know how we did it all, but we moved into our new place by the time the sun set that Monday evening. It was a miracle.

I was open to just about anything for work. I was still shoplifting- returning items, getting new ones, and then returning those items for gift receipts (a store clerk offered this to me, to my surprise and delight), which allowed me the choice of receiving cash or credit for items returned with that gift receipt. That paid the bills for a couple of months while I worked part-time jobs here and there, figuring out what I wanted to do. I went on countless interviews and started at numerous places only to quit within a week or two. Eventually, I found steady work.

Back to Mack, the "Motorcycle Man". Mack came up to visit me within the first month I arrived (when Juliet and I were still in the U District). It was apparent then that his emotional discomfort was going to be a problem for me. He visited again not too long after his first trip and stayed in our new place. I don't even remember if we had sex (I don't think so). Most of the time I wasn't sure if he was even having a good time because he didn't express much emotion. He was a pleasant guy, just not very personal or affectionate. I assumed that if something was wrong, he'd tell me. He was more reserved emotionally than almost anyone I'd ever met.

By the end of October, I was working at a telemarketing place where I met this guy named Bobby, who had a girlfriend in Greece (he's half Greek). He was cute, but I didn't think much of him. I had Mack and Bobby had his girlfriend. I wasn't interested in Bobby as more than a friend. I was actually glad that he had a girlfriend so that there wouldn't be an issue between us as friends.

One night, he invited me, his sister Ariana, Juliet and somebody else to a movie. Shortly after the movie began, he put his thumb in my mouth, which was covered in chocolate sauce from something he had, intending for me to lick it off. I was a tad bit taken aback, but it wasn't a big deal either, so I told myself. He came back to my place after the movie. We were hanging out in my room and we started kissing. One thing led to another and we were lovers for the whole month of November.

My birthday is November 10th. Bobby made that birthday a very memorable one! He was the first person to ever ask me if I was happy with him sexually (this was in the morning, after we had just had GREAT sex) and he wanted to know if there was anything more he could do to please me sexually. As I sat in my bathrobe, in complete contentment and awe, I smiled radiantly and said, "I am perfectly happy! If I think of anything later, can I let you know?" He said that was fine.

Bobby showed me what it was like to have an unselfish lover. It was absolutely wonderful!! Our feelings never turned romantic. We both understood that we were great lovers, but nothing more. His girlfriend visited for the month of December. We met and got along really well. I became close with Bobby's whole family who had just moved to Seattle from Vancouver, Canada (after living in Greece for a while and then Los Angeles). Ariana and I became best friends and she's remained one of the best friends I've ever had to this day. She and Juliet became very close too. Ariana used to stay at our place often. At times, she helped keep the peace between Juliet and I.

That Thanksgiving, I went down to Olympia (after spending the day with Bobby. Terrible, I know.) to see Mack and consider ending things with him. Sometime in October, he had gotten into a motorcycle accident and had his leg in a cast. As soon as I found out, I was on a bus for 8-12 hours and went straight to the hospital. I thought that he might be more open towards me emotionally after that whole incident.

Mack had shattered a bunch of bones in his ankle. Even then he played the "stoic" role. I couldn't take the emotional distance anymore or his sexual shyness. He was extremely self-conscious about his penis size, to the point where he wouldn't ever have sex with the lights on or allow me to please him orally, and I'd had enough. I didn't tell him all of that. I don't remember what I told him. We just stopped calling each other. We've barely spoken since. Over the years, I've called and left messages, but he never returns my calls.

I began thinking a lot about Tim around this time (December), but I was slowly getting over him (Yes, he was gay, but I was in love with him for 2 years, c'mon!). Things with Bobby were over and Maxine and I had been keeping in touch through letters. So I poured my heart out to her. She had written me a letter from school that was forthcoming about her feelings for me. I wrote her back with much passion and love in my heart. She said that she'd visit me sometime in March. I wasn't sure if she really would come, but I prepared for her arrival anyway. It kept my spirits up.

We did a cleansing at the same time. No alcohol, coffee (which I never drank), cigarettes, or pot for 30 days. It ended a few days before she came out to see me. She thought to do a cleansing as a way to prepare for her recital. I thought it was a great idea and just wanted to do it with her. I'd never heard of it before. I was eating well (for the first time in my life) and feeling good. I started a graveyard (overnight) position at a phone chat line where I was screening people's greetings for each other. I was eagerly awaiting Maxine's arrival.

I had all of these things planned to do when she got to Seattle, but she was all about just spending time with me, so we didn't do much sight seeing. She stayed for one week. She was my first and only visitor that year. As open as she was with me, I still felt her reservations. I could sense her holding back and I wasn't sure why. I did all I could to assure her that my love for her was true and that she could trust me. She kept saying that it would simply take time because she was badly hurt by her last boyfriend (the one who cheated on her). I was willing to be patient.

It was easy to adjust to Seattle. Its natural beauty is breathtaking. I found the people very easy for me to get along with, compared to people I'd encountered up until then on the east coast. There are lots of vegetarians, environmentally conscious and animal friendly people living in the northwest United States. From a child I ate less and less meat as I grew older due to the quality of the products I was exposed to in my formative years. I finally stopped eating meat altogether right before I moved to Seattle. It's a very politically aware city too. The Northwest is also the most well read region of the U.S. It offers a lot culturally for fairly cheap, if not free, which was wonderful to me.

I was finally caught shoplifting at a major department store (BAD idea) shortly after Christmas, but nothing more than a $75 fine came out of it. Since it was a misdemeanor and my first offense, it's not on my record. I tell my mom almost everything (except the things I know she'd really rather not hear about) and the idea of telling her about getting arrested was frankly too embarrassing (I eventually told her, much later). That's what made me stop. I like to feel comfortable telling anybody anything that I've done whether they agree with my choices or not. It was obvious that I didn't truly agree with what I was doing or else I wouldn't have had a problem telling anyone close to me, like mom. At times I felt like Robin Hood- robbing from "the corporate world" who ripped off people anyway. Many of my friends (and one cute waitress) reaped the rewards of my stolen goods as well. Sometimes I bought gifts for people using store credit acquired through shoplifting. I had also stopped appreciating the things I had (clothing) as much as I used too. I haven't shoplifted since.

Problems were arising between me and Juliet. We'd known each other since she was a sophomore and I was a junior at Central. We'd spent countless nights at my mom's (as well as her mom's) house having a blast! Our strongest bonds were our love for Jane's Addiction's music and Nature.

The first time Juliet was at my house, I was obsessed with the song "Summertime Rolls" (It's what made me fall in love with them). She came into my room while I was listening to it one afternoon and began singing the lyrics with me. Pretty much no one I knew liked Jane's Addiction, most certainly not like I did, except Juliet. She introduced me to Pink Floyd and helped me fall in love with Nine Inch Nails. Thanks to her and Bill, I couldn't escape appreciating Jimi Hendrix. They're all now part of my all time favorite musicians group.

Our problems weren't about music; they were mainly about insecurity (boys, body image, friendship, love). She hated introducing me to her friends because she didn't like me becoming friends with them, especially this one extremely cute boy named Tyler. He was a sweet guy from British Columbia, Canada. I always wondered if he was gay (hung around with gay men, was a "pretty boy" and so sweet and nice). We ended up kissing one night. Juliet had met him first, but she expressed no interest to me in pursuing him romantically, even though she was attracted to him. Tyler and I were hanging out a lot more than they were because of our time schedules and interests. Once we kissed, Juliet was pissed.

She got over it after a little while, but once summer came, it was all over. I'm a very sensual person and that was the VERY first summer in my life that I felt as comfortable with my body as I did then. I could wear virtually anything, even nothing, and feel good about my body. I was rollerblading a lot. I was more active in Seattle, than I'd ever been in my life, so I was more confident due to the way I felt and also being slimmer and trimmer than I'd ever known myself to be. Rollerblading 2-3 times a week in some of the most beautiful areas I'd ever seen while listening to my favorite music was a wonderful and natural high. It was an extremely freeing time in many ways.

Juliet was nowhere near where I was at that time in terms of comfort with her self inwardly or outwardly. It wasn't even so much the way she looked. We both had our "problem areas" as well as our attractive features. It boiled down to the fact that I was happy and loved myself more than she did at that time. That's what had changed so much between us. She was her own worst enemy and she took this out on her self and all those around her, as many of us do (and not realize it) when we're in that state.

It was a tough situation for us both. I loved Juliet like a sister and she was pushing me out of her life. It was awful to feel bad for feeling good around one of your best friends and lose them as a result. It was partly what I feared in feeling good around friends of mine who felt bad about their selves. I didn't want them to feel like they had to feel a certain way around me either. More than anything, I wished we could've spoken openly and honestly without emotions getting hurt or feelings turning sour, but I had no idea how to do that.

The last month we lived together (she decided to move to San Francisco, where Paula had moved about six months prior, at the end of August '97), Juliet didn't even speak to me. Her friend Britney had moved in to finish out the lease. I moved out of that fabulous place at the end of September with hopes of living in Italy as an au pair for I'd been in touch with Kate who was doing that while I was away. The friends that I had dissed in Philly before I left were on okay terms with me again. Almost all of us had spoken at some point. It was still a little awkward (broken trust), but much better. I planned to return to Philly before heading to Rome.

Rewind for just a minute, the summer of '97 was a crazy summer romantically for me! I had sex with this guy from work (sex with co-workers=BAD IDEA!) who was super arrogant (his "persona") and very good-looking. He was a writer. He flirted with me. I was young and naïve. What else can I say? Thankfully, he's an exception in my romantic repertoire; however, I do wish more men that I've been with could have been as honest as he was. I thought he (and the sex) would get better. Within a week, I knew it wouldn't, but he ended up dumping me first. It was a BIG blow to my ego.

He didn't like me talking to other guys at work because many were attracted to me. I'd give some shoulder massages at times, but I didn't think it was anything to feel threatened over. It was an eight-day relationship, but I still wish I'd dumped him first because I didn't even really like him, yet he told me, "This isn't going to work." much easier and quicker than I thought was possible for him to do. That bruise took a while to heal, but it was a good lesson for me to learn. It's the same one I've continued to relive over and over and over again:
GET TO KNOW SOMEONE <u>VERY WELL</u> BEFORE SHARING YOURSELF SEXUALLY!!!
I don't have "casual sex". Nothing is casual about ANY

relationship I have- with friends, family, my lovers, or myself. I've learned to be much more discriminating throughout the years with whom I invite closely into my life, but I still get carried away at times by my feelings. I have a tendency to believe more in people's potential without waiting, being patient and seeing just how consistent they are. I now like to see to what degree and how often their words match up with their actions.

This same summer, a few of my guy friends confessed that they were attracted to me and/or in love with me and it drove me nuts. I wasn't doing anything to lead them on (I was clearly, happily single, so I thought). I disliked being confronted with their feelings. With each of them, I felt it was pretty obvious that nothing would ever happen. One of my friends was a 65 year-old man whom I looked up to as a mentor of sorts. I didn't know what they really expected. It felt to me as if my friendship with them wasn't enough and that they didn't really care about it. I told one guy that I was a lesbian. I kept that up for almost two years.

I had a huge crush on this Spanish guy at a part-time job that I worked at in a downtown bakery. We'd flirted for a couple of months before I finally kissed him one night. He was just out for booty. He didn't get this one, but I was crushed to find out that that's all he wanted from me. A man once told me, "A man will say, do, and be anything just to get in your pants." I didn't believe him- at the time. My mind was slowly beginning to change, for too many guys whom I thought were my real friends at that time turned out not to be. Their intents weren't bad, just not platonic, or else they would still be my friends, which none of them are.

In October '97, I was back in Philly. Plans fell through with the Italian family and Kate told me that it didn't pay well, so I tossed the idea. I was living with my mom (who was awesome and understanding, but still difficult to live with after living on my own for 2 years.), deciding what to do next. I turned 21 years old that November and realized that I had been smoking cigarettes for 5 years (along with pot and drinking alcohol). So I decided to take a nice, long break- at some point.

When I turned 21, I cut my hair drastically. It was past the middle of my back, curly (the longest it had ever been) and I cut it to less than an inch all over. I always said that I'd cut it really short and then grow it really long. I didn't want to be attached to my hair. I was curious to see if I would get less attention because it was so much shorter (people often made comments about my hair). After that summer, I was ready to hide in the shadows and lay low for a bit.

I started seeing this guy named Frankie who was a friend of Maxine's. I was getting with Maxine from time to time. She lived in Philly for a semester while I was in Philly. Things weren't going too well between us though. We had different expectations of each other. I was more into her than I was Frankie. I broke things off with him first (after about a month, no sex), then with Maxine, about 2 weeks later. I wanted some time alone to figure things out. I'd never had feelings for more than one person at a time. It messed with me.

The realization that a person, such as myself, can have strong romantic feelings for more than one person at a time was a major milestone! I had already thought about it with Devon and Patrick as well as Tim and Mack, but those seemed more like transitions than co-existing feelings. The only reason that Maxine and Frankie were cool with knowing about each other was because they were friends and the opposite sex, but to me, it didn't matter. They were each a person I was romantically involved with, as if they were two men. I had to figure out what that meant to me. I was getting a clearer image of what I wanted from "romance", but it was still distorted. If I felt that way, then my partner could too. Would I be okay if they were with the same sex? I wasn't okay with double standards. It was time to get some answers before exploring romance and sexuality with my emotions any further.

Ariana didn't care much for Maxine (she'd met her when she visited Seattle), but she knew how much I cared for Maxine. When I told her that I wasn't talking to Maxine at all anymore (we'd gotten into a fight over miscommunication), she let me know that it was an ego thing. She felt I'd be happier with Maxine in my life. She was right and I knew it. That was a few days before New Years Eve. I vowed not to drink, smoke cigarettes or pot all year long. Shortly afterwards, I called Maxine. We reconciled, but things were not the same, as far as how much we trusted each other, which showed in our interactions for a while. She went back to school in early January and I figured out what I was going to do next.

Right before I left Seattle, I was working at The Green Cat Café- a vegetarian spot on Capitol Hill. It was one of the best jobs I'd had up until that point. I wondered if I could go back. Living with mom wasn't cutting it and I was ready to leave Philadelphia. The winter sucked. I abhor cold weather. I had gained 25 pounds in the span of 4-5 months and I wasn't feeling too good about myself overall. I was happy with my

sobriety though. I knew that was a good idea. It was the first time I'd
ever quit cigarettes and I did it cold turkey. I was proud of myself.
Alcohol wasn't much of a temptation aside from the occasional glass of
red wine (which finally did me in sometime in July, but only a few times
that entire year). Pot was something I knew could wait and did, until I
saw Leah for our birthdays (she's a Scorpio too).

Someone I'd met in Seattle through Juliet gave me a copy of a
book called, "Illusions" by Richard Bach. A few people had mentioned
it to me as a book I'd love, but the cover looked so cheesy, "Illusions:
The Adventures of a Reluctant Messiah" over a starry background with
a blue feather, that I had put off reading it. The time had come. I was
captivated within the first few pages. Richard Bach became my hero. I
had never loved a book so much as I had loved "Illusions". It said so
many things that I'd thought and felt and wondered about that I could
hardly believe that it was real.

The storyline made me laugh. I love intelligent books with a
sense of humor. Richard Bach's style mirrored much of my own as a
writer, so I felt. I read that book countless times. Some of the "catch
phrases" (from the "Messiah's Handbook") I'd read to various friends,
especially Maxine. I was enchanted and delighted. It was so simple, yet
profound. It's a favorite of mine to this day. It made me feel like a jedi
in training.

Around the end of March ('98) I decided to call the owner of
The Green Cat Café to see about working there again. I missed all that
Seattle offered for the little that I had and the winters weren't as harsh.
The owner said that he could have me on the schedule in a week. I was
THRILLED! I packed my bags, bought my bus ticket (that's how I got
back to Philly) and moved, for the second time, to the Emerald City.

At The Green Cat, I could eat tasty and nutritious vegetarian fare
for free. It was a favorite, local hang out, in the neighborhood where I
used to live, which was an easy area to find an apartment and the tips
there were very good for just taking orders and making espresso drinks.
It felt more like being in someone's house than in a restaurant. Every
table was unique. We played our own music, which was always different
and we had outdoor tables and chairs.

The Cat was glad to have me back and I was glad to be back! I
stayed with Ariana for a few weeks until I moved into my old room in
my old apartment that I shared with Juliet. My friend Andy had moved
into our old place with a friend of his and was going to Europe for the
summer, so I paid his rent while he was gone. It worked out perfectly! It

was only a 15-minute walk away from The Green Cat. It was summer again. I was in Seattle and I was beaming!! I moved into a house with a co-worker, his fiancé and her daughter. That didn't work for long. I felt more like a guest than a roommate, let alone friend, so I moved after only two months there.

I moved to Alki, which is a beachfront neighborhood in West Seattle. It's one of my favorite places in the world. The place I found was only $300/mo. It was a living situation in a house with this guy who placed an ad in the local paper. It was cheap and beautiful, but the guy was off! I didn't expect to be there much or for long and I didn't realize he was truly wacko until too late. I was definitely a little too willing to give people the benefit of the doubt (I learned my lesson here!).

Sometime during my first week there, he came to my door one night to see if I was "okay". He was stark naked with a rock hard penis, just standing there at my bedroom doorway! I told him that I was fine, bid him goodnight and closed the door (there was no lock). I was on the phone with someone at the time. Perhaps that saved me. I don't know. He was a small, older guy, but he had some strength and liked to drink. Fortunately, he just turned around and went back to bed. I was packed and gone the next afternoon. He kept $600 of mine that he never gave back. Lesson learned.

I was not happy about that situation AT ALL! The financial loss was harsh, but I was happy that nothing worse happened. I stayed with Ariana until she couldn't take me anymore (a little less than a month). The day that she told me that I had to find another place to stay (we were such different people in our homes during that time and it was a one bedroom.), I found a terrific studio right around the corner from the Cat.

Upon the suggestion of a co-worker, I went to see this place during my lunch break. I loved it! The landlord let me move in that day with only $333. I didn't even have that, but my boss/the owner at the Cat gave me the money that I was short. I slept in the very first place I'd ever had all to myself that night and I thanked the universe humbly and deeply for orchestrating such SPLENDID events!

There was one problem, however…somehow, in November, with hardwood floors, I had fleas. I DO NOT like fleas. I get paranoid about seeing them everywhere. I begin to think that every black speck is a flea and they multiply so fast! They lasted almost a month and it drove me insane. After my fleas were all gone, I finally settled into my brand new, beautiful place.

By this time, I was the front of the house manager at the Cat. I had been working for a couple of months and was considering going back to school (I'd attended Penn State for 3 semesters and felt ready to finish my degree). I had enrolled for a quarter at the Community College in Seattle the year before (in the spring of '97) and liked it more than I thought I would. Students were of all ages. My teachers were thought provoking and cool. It was within walking distance of my house and it had a gym that was part of the membership. I also loved that on the main street in front of the school, there's a bad-ass metal sculpture of Jimi Hendrix on his knees playing guitar.

Working at the Cat would've been too much while I was in school, so I gave my 2 weeks notice and began looking for another job. That very same week, I answered an ad for an Internet manager. I loved technology and had no experience, but they specifically asked for females and I am a female! When I called, I found out that it was only 2 blocks from my place and they started at $11/hr. I could hardly believe it. It seemed destined, even though I wasn't clear as to what they were looking for. I went in for the interview and got the job, another miracle for which I was very thankful.

As an internet manager at this particular company, it was my responsibility to make sure that all of the performers were signed in and out correctly, chat with customers via the website, keep track of the people who logged in and to make it look like our feed was live by keeping an eye on which girl was where on site and on camera. This was an adult Internet site. Our location was the "live section" of a well-known site at that time.

During the day and swing shifts, the managers filmed individual people masturbating as well as couples simulating sex, so sometimes it was live, other times we played tapes. All of this (manager's duties) was done from one room called the control room where customers could view the manager as well. Our backs were generally to the camera and it was dark in there most of the time I worked.

Everyone (except the "couples" people) was in a separate room. The couples couldn't show penetration in any way, so they didn't have to have sex, but some did and when they did it was up to the manager to either tell them to change their position or to zoom far enough away that it wasn't clear to see penetration.

The girls had 4 rooms to choose from: the bedroom, the health club, the 2-girl (2 shower heads, usually only one girl) shower, and the dungeon. The couples and guys only had one room. We weren't allowed to show ejaculation either. Most people faked their orgasms aside from a couple of the girls and a few couples.

My boss was a pill popper with erratic mood swings, so I did my best to stay away from her. My main shift was from 3am-11am. I hardly ever saw my boss because she usually didn't show up until noon. It was an excellent job when I was there by myself, which was most of the time. Performers didn't perform during my shift. I just put in and took out the videotapes.

Sometimes I watched movies or got on the Internet in another office that I wasn't supposed to be in where a friend of mine worked next door. The bickering, backstabbing, and all around distrust between co-workers was awful, but oddly enough, most of us got along pretty well. It was the upper management that was the worst. Oftentimes, I filled in for managers during other shifts for I lived the closest, but I didn't like to do it too much because it put me at risk of getting caught up in the gossip mill, which was always some new drama.

We had guest porn stars come every other week. Some were cool women. I actually kept in touch with a couple of the performers from that place once I left. I received one of the best books I've ever read, "Anatomy of the Spirit" from one of the performers there. It's a mainstay in my life. Another performer is one of my best friends. I was in the hospital room for the birth of her second child and video taped the whole thing. She and another friend once fell asleep on camera while masturbating- separately, not together.

I never did go back to school. I didn't want to work at all while attending classes and I couldn't afford to take time off. I saw "The Matrix" that spring ('99) and decided that it was about time I got my butt (literally) in shape! I was pushing 160 pounds. I was only 5'3" and the weight wasn't from muscle, so I joined a gym.

A guy named Brad that I'd met the year before became a friend of mine through teaching me about reconditioning myself. He helped me to consciously create my life. He put together a 12-week course, similar to Landmark (which I knew nothing about then) and I learned a great deal about life and myself.

Ever since I'd dated Mack, I was an incessant reader. I'd take out 5-20 books out of the library at a time. I was learning a great deal within a short amount of time. I had plenty of time to do whatever I wanted at the Internet place, so I absorbed the information that my friend Brad was teaching me and recommending to me very easily on a mental level, however it was a different story on an emotional and spiritual level.

Between reading "Anatomy of the Spirit" and doing Brad's course (which I did twice because I dropped out after the third week the first time), I was a bit overwhelmed with all of the change I knew I needed to make in my life in order to feel fulfilled on every level of my being. True happiness is what I was in search of, but I didn't realize that it would take so much work! At times, it was extremely daunting.

It was the end of April ('99) and I had begun to feel pretty darn good about myself (after not feeling so good for a while) when I walked into a frame store one spring afternoon, to have a painting of mine framed. It was my very first. I had painted it while living with Juliet ('97). It was my representation of true love. I had plans to go to Spain in June to visit Maxine for a month. It was to be my first time leaving the country. I heard this guy somewhere in the store talking with a thick Spanish accent. I was curious about him just by the way he sounded, but I went ahead and walked out of the store. After I stepped outside for just a second, something made me turn right back around and go back in. Don't ask me what! I was in my workout clothes, not looking cute at all! I later saw I had an earring missing too. Reason went out the window.

I went up to this man and asked him if his accent was Spanish. I barely saw him before. When I got up close to him, I could barely believe how handsome and beautiful he was. I probably wouldn't have approached him otherwise. He was extremely nice which just sealed it for me. He was STUNNING! We talked about getting together and practicing Spanish. He gave me his phone number and said, "Make sure you call me! Okay?" He said that a few times. In my head I thought, "Don't you worry! Hell couldn't stop me from calling you!"

When I left the shop, I felt high. I wanted to run home and write poetry! I was CHEESIN'!! I told the girls at work about him that night and called him the very next day. His accent was so thick, and his English so poor, that it was hard to have a conversation. I questioned my patience, for it was that bad, until I saw him again. We had made plans to hang out the next day. I was ecstatic, but I planned to keep my cool. I hadn't had sex in over 2 years at that point (since the 8 day guy who bruised my ego). It had also taken this long to sort out my feelings regarding loving more than one person at a time.

I hadn't kissed anyone in over a year and a half, and then came Raphael, an archangel indeed, at least, to me. He was late to meet me. I was annoyed, but once I saw him again, I didn't even care. We were like 2 little kids. He has a tattoo covering his whole back. It's a dragon's head with a third eye and the number 22 above it. I was 22 years old. It was his favorite number. He was 22, turning 23 in less than 2 months. I was born in the year of the dragon. There were too many coincidences between us for me to ignore the profundity of the situation. Even though we barely knew each other, I felt strongly connected to him on multiple levels.

Before I left Seattle the first time on the autumnal equinox-September 22nd, I got the outline of a snake biting it's own tail in the shape of infinity (vertically) tattooed in black ink along my entire back. The next year I returned to the same artist on the same day and finished it. The first visit took 45 minutes. The second visit took close to 4 hours, for all of the scales and shading had to be done. The artist's sister called after the scales and during the shading. It had been a long time since they'd spoken, so they talked for a good half an hour.

That day I was menstruating. Some artists won't tattoo a woman if they know that, due to sensitivity and loss of blood (I didn't say anything). So when my artist began to work on me again after my back became tender and sore from the break, I wasn't sure I'd be able to take the pain until he finished. I had brought my walkman with a brilliant mix of songs that I'd made to keep me blissed out while he carved into my back. This degree of pain took my meditation practice to a whole new level. I breathed as evenly and calmly as I could. I closed my eyes and focused solely on the music and let it take me away.

My body was in that chair being tattooed, enduring tremendous pain, but if I paid attention every single second to my thoughts and feelings using the music to help focus, I was soaring in the sky, dancing around a great, big full moon. I was the whispers of clouds and the stardust of the galaxies. I was the wind as well as ether and the universe was my playground. If I lost focus even for one second, I was back in that chair again, so I paid VERY CLOSE attention to EXTREME feelings of love and deep pleasure every single second that I was under the needle, until it stopped. I've never once regretted it.

Both of our tattoos were done in black ink only, with minimal designs. I rarely meet people with tattoos that are anything like mine, so meeting him so soon after getting mine was a blatant sign and I was paying close attention in those days. He's a Cancer. I'm a Scorpio. We both were looking to have some sort of career in film, television and/or modeling (behind the camera more for me), which I had just started to consider. We knew very little about the industry. He was my muse. I got SO much inspiration and knowledge from just being around him.

I found out that Raphael is Argentinean. I always wanted to visit

South America. He had already been traveling abroad for a year and a half. He was due to return home in 2 weeks. He missed his family a lot. I wanted to travel anywhere and everywhere with him. I wanted to get to know him, help him, support and encourage him. I wanted him to be in my life forever. A few hours later, the same day I first hung out with him, I proposed marriage to him.

He wasn't sure if I was serious. I assured him that I was. We planned to marry in Buenos Aires after I arrived in the fall. We didn't get into details, but we were excited. His body was UNREAL! He was a rock climber, snowboarder and worked out often at the gym. I loved his upper body. All of him was exquisite. He took great care of himself in every which way. I'd never been with a man like him before. It wasn't all about his looks either. They were distracting actually. I didn't want him to think that I felt all that I did just because he was gorgeous.

He came to my apartment a couple of days later and kissed me almost immediately. I didn't plan to kiss him so soon (I tried to exercise the "getting to know you" lesson), but he was HARD to resist. I didn't have sex with him though. I still wanted to take things slow physically. After a week, I told him that I don't want to do anything for an indefinite period of time (this has become my "trademark"). I had another good reason for taking things slow.

Towards the end of my first year in Seattle, I participated in this study for the use of the birth control shot known as Depo Provera. Due to regular gynecological visits, I'd learned that I had acquired a sexually transmitted disease known as Human Papillomavirus (HPV). It's commonly known among women now, but it was just beginning to be talked about when I was treated.

There was no way to know what partner passed it to me seeing as it can be passed even using condoms. I told all my past lovers anyway. What might happen (not in all cases) is that the infected person has warts on their genitals (usually when the body's under a lot of stress), in which case they can be frozen or burned off. It's possible to be aware of it and unknowingly pass the virus on to someone else though. There is no cure. I had to be treated before. It wasn't fun, but it wasn't horrible either. It's good motivation to keep my health in check and to be careful with whom I share my body.

Raphael was the first person that I was nervous about telling I had HPV because I liked him so much. At first he thought I said HIV, so he was relieved, but still confused. I printed him out a bunch of information so that he was aware of the facts about it, but his English was not good enough to read that kind of material. Seeing as he was leaving so soon and I wanted his trust more than anything, it was an easy decision for me to decide to simply wait to have sex until a later, more appropriate time. I'm not one for quick experiences. I like to revel in the things I enjoy.

We thought it'd be easier to process all of his immigration papers here, in the U.S., instead of Argentina. He extended his stay until June 3rd. We married on May 22, 1999 on Alki Beach in West Seattle. My friend Dean (whom I'd met at the chat line place in '97) was the minister. A bunch of our friends came and had a wonderful time. The Olympic Mountains were out (a majestic mountain range in the west), the sun was shining and my good friend Babs made me a vegan, organic, coconut cake that was out of this world! I was eating only vegan and organic foods for the month of May to see how I felt eating that way. I also fasted twenty-four hours beforehand.

I planned the wedding and left the honeymoon up to Raphael. He had friends to help him. We had decided to go camping before that night, so he had time to figure things out. I ate some mushrooms that a friend had given me, on the way there thinking he knew exactly where he was going. Nope! As the sunset, we got more and more lost in the pitch-black darkness. I was tripping fairly hard and just wanted to get somewhere. I was ready to go back to my apartment. He was determined to find a campground. We didn't argue about it though, which showed me a lot for it was a stressful situation.

Thankfully, someone was kind enough to drive us right to a camping area (a few people told us how easy it was, gave us directions and we'd get lost again). I gave that guy a great, big hug before he left. When we arrived at our site, I got out of the car, wrapped myself in a sleeping bag and immediately snuggled with this tree while Raphael built a fire. I learned one of the greatest lessons I've ever learned in my whole life, that night.

The night of my honeymoon, I (my spirit/being) was among the stars looking at earth. I knew I didn't have to use my human body anymore. I didn't want to go back to living on earth as I was. I knew I couldn't just leave my body in the woods with Raphael. It was clear that I had more things that were important to do on earth before I left my body for good. Before I "came back", I asked my family of love (the stars/beings/energies around me), "How can I remember all that I learned/saw tonight and keep this feeling with me all the time?" They said, "Shhh…just be quiet and listen. (silence) We are ALWAYS here. It is you who leave us."

A tremendous feeling of peace permeated me. I was no longer afraid of dying from that moment forward. I haven't felt lonely or alone since. I can remember that feeling of immense love to this day. I do my best not to let myself forget it.

Raphael understood most of these things (or so I thought) when I explained them to him. His English was always getting better and I had learned some Spanish (I knew very little). He understood me in ways few people that I had met up to that point did. We didn't do anything sexual at all the night of our honeymoon either. We talked; we cuddled and fell asleep in the back of his truck (it was cold outside and comfortable in the truck). He left for Argentina June 1st. I left for Spain June 3rd. The plan was for me to meet up with Raphael in Buenos Aires sometime in the fall, live there until our paperwork finished processing and come back to the States together.

Our marriage had nothing to do with sexual monogamy. I wrote our own wedding vows and made sure that he at least understood those words clearly. He knew that I was attracted to women (I had kissed a few at this point) and he was fine with that. It's the guys I wondered about. However, I'm not attracted to that many men. It's rare for me to meet someone I'm compatible with AND attracted to enough to invite into my life sexually. Men tend to be a lot more comfortable with women being with other women than with other men. Since I'm not casual with my relations, I had a feeling that at some point, it might be an issue. I was willing to give my first open relationship an honest shot though.

I was monogamous with Raphael for the first year of our relationship, but it wasn't because I promised to be, which I like. That way you know I'm with you every moment that I am because I want to be, not because I have to be. Raphael was never monogamous with me. I never expected him to be. As long as he didn't sleep with just anyone and used protection, I was not bothered in the slightest. I wasn't having sex with his fine self, why not someone else? Honesty, to this extent, was very difficult for him though. He was not at all used to a woman like me, especially with him having lived so much of his life in South America.

The first month or so that we were apart, I missed him terribly. He was my partner through and through. I strongly felt his presence and absence. I had loads of fun in Spain, but I couldn't wait to get back to

Seattle. Maxine wanted to hook up in Spain (she was the last person I'd kissed before Raphael), but I didn't feel like being with anyone sexually at the time. We were together once shortly after I arrived and I knew it was better not to be sexually involved with her at that point. I didn't plan well for Spain. I didn't have a lot of money to travel around, so I stayed in and around Malaga.

Maxine introduced me to the friends she'd made during her 7 weeks there prior to my arrival. Kayla was a friend of Maxine's, from Finland, who was studying in Spain. She was the most adorable person I'd ever met! I loved her British accent and sense of humor. Many of us got along fabulously. I was anxious to get back to work, my apartment, my computer and friends though.

As much as I enjoyed Malaga, the Mediterranean and its beaches, the Northwest is a more naturally beautiful region, lush with life that I longed for and food catered to health freaks like I had become. In the center of town, in Malaga, was one of the best vegetarian places I've ever dined. It was a fantastic experience! It reminded me of the movie "Like Water for Chocolate" and everyone with us that night (around 8 of us) felt that way. I'm very glad that I went. Before leaving, the chef kissed me on the mouth because I expressed so much love for his food.

Before Raphael left, I befriended a close girl friend of his named Tiffany. She and I were obviously attracted to each other. We constantly emailed back and forth while I was in Spain. She was married to a Columbian man, one of Raphael's friends. When I returned from Spain, we made out one night, but then she and one of my best friend's, Tom (who stayed with me for a month, then lived with me for three), ended up hooking up and getting serious pretty quickly. He fell hard for her. It was a torrid and erratic love affair. Tiffany loved her husband, but they both dated other people and Tom didn't like that. He grew to dislike her over time, as did I. Tom and I are still very good friends.

My breaking point with Tiffany was when I found out that she and Raphael had had sex in Argentina a few times when she visited him for 3 months before my arrival. It surprised me that they hadn't, before I found out. I didn't care that they had sex, it's the fact that both of them talked to me repeatedly, asking questions about the other to me due to all kinds of weird tension between them, yet neither of them had the balls to be straight with me. It was ridiculous.

The worst was that I found out through a friend of mine that used to be friends with both of them and he didn't tell me until after I came back to the States. I gave them no reason to lie to me. It made my trust towards them plummet. By the time I returned from Argentina, I was ready to divorce Raphael for other reasons anyway. In my decision to move to Argentina, I gave up my apartment, my job, and my life, as I knew it. I returned with very little financially, but I'd gained an immeasurable amount inwardly.

Shortly before I left Seattle for Argentina, I met this woman named Bria who was married to a famous author that I adore (he would get mad if I used his name without his permission). This happened right before I left for Philadelphia (I spent a month there before I moved to Buenos Aires), in September '99. We were enchanted with one another.

Bria was WAY more open than her husband. He was so paranoid about people. I understood and didn't care that much because it was her that was my main interest anyway. I loved her husband's writings and wished that he was cooler, but he's the same character in his books as well. The way we met was through his website. I sent in a question (after going to the one and only book reading/signing I've ever attended) and she (his new wife, not the one he wrote about in his books) responded to it. I was happy just to know that she existed. She was a radiant, powerful and lovely being. I had no idea that the author was no longer with the woman he wrote about. The love he waxed on about in several books was part of what fed me on the existence of true love and soul mates. 'Twas amazing to learn which aspects were true and which were fiction. His books were all works of fiction, but ones that had strong resonance in "everyday life".

Visiting Philly that fall was sublime!! I was happy, grounded, and spent almost all of my money, but not frivolously. I was tired of worrying about what life would be like without money. My fears were at an all time low. I was totally into the idea of the universe taking care of me. I was testing the waters, seeing for myself what was true in theory and what was factual. I was afraid of not having enough money. I was about to find out what would happen if I were completely broke and dependent on others. I hadn't lived that way since before I was 18 years old. It was hard not to be nervous. I worked on my faith that things would work out for the best as long as I followed my heart.

Bria saw me in Seattle the night before I left for Buenos Aires and asked me how much I had on me. I told her that I had $5. She gave me $50- all that she had on her. She wanted to do all she could to help me. I knew I'd be okay, no matter what. She said that she'd visit and that she'd help me find a job through her husband's book publishing company that had an office in Buenos Aires. That gave me hope, which meant a lot to me then, for I was about to begin a life in a foreign country where I didn't speak the language, being solely dependent on someone I'd known for only one month of my life.

Upon my arrival in Buenos Aires, my hopes were high, but that didn't last long. Every day was a struggle and a high. Raphael's mom was like an ANGEL and his brother was like the devil (he was nicknamed "Fede Krueger" at one point by Raphael's friends). The babysitter was one of the most compassionate and kind out of most of the people I met there. She was comparable to the friends I made- two whom I still keep in touch. For 12 hour days of babysitting (she was 16 or 17), she only made $2 or so a day. I said to her, "Tu eres un angel!" all the time, which means, "You are an angel!"

Raphael's mom was living in a small, one-bedroom apartment with little furniture. His 5-year-old brother Fede was a true TERROR! I would pray he'd go to daycare every day, for he'd cry and yell most of the day if he stayed home. I slept during the day, stayed up all night writing and stayed out in the evening until I was sure he was asleep. I slept on the floor with a bunch of comforters because his mom only had one mattress, that she offered to us, but I would not take the only bed in the whole house! The comforters were fine. It was hot. I was sheltered and fed. I had my whole life open to me and for the first time, I thought about what I'd love to do regardless of how much money I made doing it.

None of the aforementioned things were that bad. Even the missing toilet seat in the bathroom or the mosquito larvae in the tap water were cool in comparison to two of Raphael's grown, obnoxious, male friends showing up unannounced 2 weeks after my arrival. They really tested my patience and love to no end!! They were only going to stay a week, then it became two. They ended up staying for 5 weeks!!! Three grown people sleeping on the living room floor for 5 weeks had to stress his mom out. They were so inconsiderate. I think they mainly used his mom's house as a free place to stay. I did as well, but it was so that I could make a life for myself there too and I was nice and considerate, at least.

One day, Raphael's mom brought Fede home a kitten- poor thing. That kitten was my savior! She had fleas, worms at one point, and that little boy tormented her, I'm sure. I loved her so much! I knew her name before Fede did. I called her Samantha and he called her Piccachu. I'd never called her Samantha aloud, yet one day I heard their mom calling her Sammy. Yup, her name had changed within days, to Samantha, without explanation. Raphael said that his brother just called her Samantha one day instead. There was also a turtle that walked around constantly pushing things (including me) out of its way.

I was broke. I had no privacy, but at least I had my music, books, paints, and my journals. During that time is when I first considered publishing my journals. I rewrote an entire one with hopes of publishing it. When I sent it to Bria to see if she could help, she suggested fictionalizing it and turning it into a story, but that simply didn't appeal to me, so I put down the idea and decided to come back to it later, for I needed to start making money really soon!

How long I was to stay in Buenos Aires was always up in the air. After about three months, my relationship with Raphael was rocky. He worked 12-hour days and liked partying a lot more (not that he partied often) than I did. I made some very good friends, but I couldn't find work and I'd grown tired of being broke. An acquaintance from Seattle (one I'd told that I was a lesbian) had wired me $300 for Christmas. He had some serious cash and is the only person who did that, once. He liked me a lot. Once that money was just about gone, winter there was approaching and Raphael was around less and less, so I decided it was time to leave contemplating a move for better work.

I returned to Philadelphia on Valentine's Day, 2000. I intended to surprise my mom at home, for I told no one that I was returning. I called Paula from New York and asked her to meet me at the airport. She picked me up and took me downtown first. We stopped and saw Dick (her ex), who was working at a restaurant. He wanted to see Bill, as did I, and I never made it home that night. I had sex with Bill for the first time that night. We had kissed years ago, for one week, a year before the orgy on his parents' bed, but it wasn't anything memorable.

We both thought the other was attractive, but we weren't into each other romantically, which I loved. I appreciated my guy friends that could be just friends with me. Bill told me before I left for Argentina that he wanted to have sex with me. I told him that the cigarette smoking was not for me and that I'd consider it if he ever quit, but that night, I was ready to go! I had finally decided to have sex with Raphael a few times (shortly) before I left, but it was not the experience I was looking for any of those times. I trusted Bill and his love more than Raphael's at that point. I was ready to welcome sex with others back into my life and Bill made it easy to do this.

By the end of that week though, Bill began falling in love with a woman from work that ended up being one of the greatest loves of his life. This didn't upset me at all, for Bill was one of my best friends. I was happy to see him falling in love for the first time, especially with someone as healthy as she was. Bill had many self-destructive tendencies that were some of the biggest reasons I'd never considered Bill seriously as a romantic interest. I always told him, "If you don't treat yourself well consistently, how are you going to consistently treat me well?"

Raphael could not return to the States until his paperwork finished processing in Argentina. We didn't know how long that would take. Some said up to a year, some said up to two years. I changed our address from Seattle to Philly as well, which didn't help. I didn't even care at that point. I still loved him. I was just fed up with working so hard to attain the degree of intimacy that I craved with him only to feel like I'd barely gotten anywhere with him emotionally over the past year. He would let me in at times and in ways, and then be completely distant. I didn't like that.

During my last week in Buenos Aires, I kissed two men. This guy named Giorgio who lived in the neighborhood adored me. He was a big Prince fan (as am I). I gave him a few cds before I left. He did anything I wanted him to do. Thankfully, for him, I'm kind, as was he, which is one of the reasons I liked him so much. He made me laugh a lot as well. His English was virtually non-existent, but he loved being around me anyway. He helped me become really good with my Spanish. We only hung out a few times, but those times were wonderful.

On the airplane, I kissed this man I'd met in the airport, while flying from Buenos Aires to NYC. He wanted to have sex with me in the bathroom on the airplane. I was not joining the mile high club that day! I did let him bring me to orgasm twice though- using his right AND left hands (separately)! I was IMPRESSED!! We had the entire middle row of a half empty plane to ourselves. I was listening to Sarah McLachlin on my discman. I didn't do anything the entire time but receive immense pleasure from that man. It was awesome! I give him a lot of credit. That was the only time I've ever been with a married man. (I care now, before I didn't). He showed me pictures of his wife and kids before he asked to kiss me, which I wasn't expecting at all. I didn't care then that he was married, for I saw it as his karma, not mine. I wouldn't do it again, nor have I since.

Right before the plane landed, I got my period (instant karma). I had a 10-hour delay at JKF airport with NO ASPIRIN and excruciating cramps. (From heaven to hell.) I had no money either to buy ANY thing! It's a miracle that I made it as far as I did. It seemed to take forever, but finally, I made it to Philly and that night is when I had sex with Bill. I know. It was one of the craziest 24 hours I've ever lived.

Being back in the United States made me feel on top of the world! In Argentina, my dollar did not go further than it did here and I wasn't making any money. I was grateful for EVERY THING, especially all of the free things that this country offers. Many parts of the U.S. are very clean in comparison to Buenos Aires or Malaga, Spain, particularly in Seattle. Seattle also has free Internet access at the library, where the computers are so much faster than ones I'd pay $5/hr for overseas. I missed my mountain ranges, blue water (a major river in Buenos Aires was brown, like dirt) and fresh air.

Time between mid-February to mid-May in Philadelphia seemed to drag on. During those three months, I was doing my best to only do work that was in line with my deepest beliefs. The closest I came to keeping a job that I liked was landscaping. That lasted two weeks. It simply didn't pay enough for all the hours and physical labor that I invested of myself. It started to get hot in Philly. I was itching to travel, missing the plethora of good paying jobs that Seattle offers and dreaming of its landscape. It was time to move back.

My weight was heavier than I wanted it to be (again, not from muscle), but I was extremely content with my life in general. Dean let me stay with him until I got back on my feet financially. I hardly worked at all in Philly those three months, so I went to Seattle broke. The Internet place had spoiled me rotten. It was tough finding any job that compared in terms of hours, pay, ease and enjoyment. I knew that my time there wouldn't last, but I had a hard time moving on from the place. My old boss at the Internet place welcomed me back with open arms. I knew I could always leave later.

Within a week of my return to Seattle, I was smitten again! This time I was knocked off my feet even more than I had been with Raphael. I saw this guy walking down the street and I immediately thought, "out of my league". He was "sleek", "urban", "polished, and yet casual" from afar. I was in the frame of mind where I was determined to do things even more if I was afraid of them. I knew this guy's rejection wouldn't be the end of me, so I followed him to his bus stop (I was waiting at my own bus stop to go to a job interview). Thankfully, his stop was only a half block away.

I went right up to him and said, "Hi, My name is Kristyn and I'd like to hear what it is that you think about." (or something to that effect). I could hardly believe the whole situation myself, but there I was saying these words to a complete stranger that I approached on the street. When I saw up close (I wear glasses, but don't usually have them) how F-I-N-E he was, I could barely keep my composure. Being nearsighted, I never trust my judgment of someone's appearance until they're within six feet of me. He ROCKED my world!

He stood there a minute, and then asked me if I'd like to have a drink with him in the coffee shop at the corner (a big, corporate one, but nice). He held the door open for me and offered to buy my drink. I was ready to die- right then and there (because he was SUCH a gentleman, which I LOVE)! I did my best to remain calm which was a huge struggle. I eyed his clothes, shoes, hair and face, and then I hoped he was gay. I just wasn't prepared to be THAT attracted to someone who could even POSSIBLY be attracted to me. The sun was shining. I had money and a good job, in a beautiful city that I loved and I was at a coffee shop with someone whom I'd just met, who was one of the most intriguing men I'd ever encountered, talking about life. It's the simple things.

We spent the next two hours in the café talking about all kinds of things before we left to catch our buses (I blew off the interview). I gave him my email address, not knowing if I'd ever hear from him again and we hugged before departing. I didn't even care if he emailed me. What he had given me was enough. The next day he sent me an email with his cell phone number. I DIED! Again.

My problem with people like him (attractive to your average woman and nice to your average person) is that I always think I'm going to mess things up somehow (I mean, I am a strange one!) and I'm just enjoying my time with them until it gets to the point where they don't like me anymore. It's easier for me to let go in the beginning, so every step forward only makes me more nervous. That's why I prefer to say everything right away that I think someone will have a problem with, in regards to my life. I don't care for any "unpleasant surprises".

His name was Joshua. It was so cute to me how "normal" he seemed. He had simple dreams and goals, at least compared to mine, for he had lived a crazy life up until recently. He dreamed of backyard barbeques with friends, having a boat to take out on the weekends and living well, but simply. He worked at a major hotel, saving money while living with his parents so that he could get out of debt and start his own business. He was 23 years old and had already done so much with his life.

At the café, I told him everything that I thought would scare him away. I said that I was in love with him (as I am with all things, to various degrees) and that I was married. He handled those things pretty well. I was digging what I was getting to know about him. He helped expand my horizons in ways I hadn't yet imagined. It surprised me that he said that he really wanted a boat. No one I'd met around my age had ever mentioned boats before. Seattle has lakes in and around the city. I've noticed them more over the years and would like one myself.

As much as I liked Joshua, I was totally comfortable and happy just hanging out with him doing whatever. It was nice that he wasn't freaked out by me and that we had such enjoyable times together. One of the first times we hung out was at the movie theater. We saw "Being John Malkovich". He had already seen it before and took me because it was about to leave the theaters and I wanted to see it. It was late and kind of far, yet he insisted on going. His kindness, wit and considerate mannerisms were all so alluring. I could barely stand to sit next to him in our seats because I felt like I was making love with his soul without any conscious effort.

A couple of weeks later, I decided to tell Joshua that I was attracted to him, just to clear the air. I had already been free with my compliments via email. One day I had even taken a box of gourmet chocolates to his job because I felt like it. I told him (via email) that he was better looking than Brad Pitt or Johnny Depp. I also said that since he smoked cigarettes and I no longer did, it deters my attraction, which was a good thing. I told him it's so nasty to me to kiss someone who smokes when I don't, unless I'm drunk. I pretty much told him all of this not having any idea what he'd say or do next, but I wasn't looking for him to quit cigarettes for the sake of my attraction. I accepted the fact that we'd just be friends. I do not mind looking without touching. He was a feast for all of my senses.

I didn't hear anything from him for a few days. When he did call, he made no mention of the email. It was a brief conversation, nothing major. He called me again that Friday (I sent the email the Saturday before) asking what I was doing that night. It was 11pm. I was hanging out with a guy I had met earlier in the week. I had no interest in him, even as a friend (which became apparent throughout the night), so I told Joshua to come pick me up. I had a few hours to spend with him before I had to be at work at 3am.

We stopped by a supermarket before going to his friend's place somewhere in the neighborhood where I worked. While walking down one of the aisles, Joshua casually mentioned that he quit smoking. I was walking a little behind him, half paying attention, when I stopped dead in my tracks. I thought, "Wait! How am I going to control myself now???" I composed myself and continued to walk, as best I could.

He went on to say that he quit smoking for Father's Day because his dad had always given him a hard time about it. I questioned his honesty (not aloud), but I had more important things to consider at the time- such as, "How am I going to get through the night without pouring my whole self onto this man??" He was handsome, funny, easy going and kind- a combination that makes me weak- and I truly wanted to platonically befriend him, however, I wasn't sure that would be the case any longer. I became greatly aroused and concerned all at once.

We went to his friend's place. He had a friend who was in the process of moving out of his apartment, wasn't sleeping there and said that it was okay for us to chill there since neither of us had our own place to be alone together. No one was there from the moment we arrived. I did think that he might've had "other intentions", but he was so relaxed and chill, I didn't expect anything either. We talked for 2 hours (no drinking or smoking anything). It was seriously hard to think that he would be attracted to me that way. Spending time with him was easy and fantastic no matter what we did.

During one of our walks, while hanging out a previous time, I had given him a shoulder massage. He told me that he used to give his girlfriends massages all the time because each of them had severe back problems. I mainly just wanted his hands on me at that point, so I asked him for a massage. By then, it was a little after 2 am. I lied down on an air mattress and raised my shirt to my neck (bra fastened). He knelt over me and started to massage my back.
He wasn't very good, but he only did it for a few minutes before he kissed my back with a little kiss. I wasn't sure what to do. I did not expect him to do that! He didn't seem like the type to initiate anything sexual. So I just lied there. He began massaging me again, for maybe a minute, and then he kissed my back again- another peck. I turned around while I sat up, gave him a funny look of confusion and disbelief and said, "So... does this mean I can kiss you??" and then he kissed me...

O   MY   GOD!!!

If I could relive ANY time in my life again, it would DEFINITELY be that night, in that house. That boy's energy knocked my socks off…(a moment of reflection, please).

Joshua looked intoxicated!! I'm sure I did too. I'm sure I did too. His eyes were rolling back in his head. I could NOT stop smiling!! He would say things like, "Every time you smile, it turns me on so much." It was one of the most sensual, beautiful, passionate, and blissful experiences of my life. I do my best to keep its memory engraved in my mind forever, for it's one of the most direct and sober encounters with a state of undeniable and immeasurable bliss I've ever experienced.

Joshua looked down at my body once while I was lying on the bed with just my skirt on and said, "You have SUCH a woman's body!" with a conviction and fervor that I hadn't felt since Bobby (and this was 10 times more). It was the perfect combination of sweet sensuality, wild abandon and pure innocence. 'Twas a taste of heaven on earth.

Work was waiting though, so I attempted to stop kissing him, but EVERY touch felt so FREAKIN' GOOD!! It was extremely tough to stop. We mainly kissed for that whole hour and a half. No type of sex was ever a serious consideration- at least not for that night. He'd go to the bathroom, splash cold water on his face, we'd say we were leaving and end up lost in each other's energy all over again as soon as we got close to one another. That happened repeatedly. We went from the wall, to the bed, to the chair, back to the wall before we FINALLY left. I was an hour and a half late for work. I figured that whomever was there would understand and be fine with it once I told them what happened.

Joshua drove me to work and we kissed some more in the car. It was 4:30 am by then. My co-worker, who couldn't leave until I arrived, thankfully, wasn't upset. I didn't hear from Joshua again for three days. I'd emailed and called him with no return messages until Sunday. He came by Dean's to pick me up the next day to hang out. We drove around talking. He broke all ties with me. To this day I'm still not exactly sure why. He was an active member of AA (sober 6 months), which discourages romantic liaisons within the first year of recovery. He said that he was busy and was feeling like he was getting sidetracked from important matters in his life. I thought that meant we would see each other less. I realize now that it meant we wouldn't be seeing each other at all anymore.

I didn't want to push him, so I told him to take his time and do his thing, but then I emailed him almost every day. I had constant access to computers at work. I thought it was a "safe" way to communicate. He grew tired of my emails because he began getting tons of junk mail due to the links I would send him from various websites. I sent him two letters in the mail as well. No response. I did my best to remain positive about the situation because I couldn't understand why we at least couldn't be friends. We got along SO well before we kissed! I wasn't ready to just let that go, but I had to. He already did.

So every once in a while, I'd email him. A couple of months later, I called him to see how he was doing. He sounded well. I wasn't doing so great at the time (late August '00), but it was nice to hear his voice. We talked for about an hour. I emailed him again a few months later and he mentioned getting together and talking, but nothing came of it.

After living with Dean, I sublet an apartment for the month of July because Giorgio from Argentina bought a plane ticket to visit me for a week in July. That was very difficult, for Giorgio's feelings only grew stronger, whereas, my feelings had lessened, especially having just kissed Joshua. Giorgio and I didn't kiss or anything. His visit was not a good one, but we made the best of it.

It was hard saving the money for my next place and figuring out where I could live and with whom. I stayed with Juliet, who was living with Leah at that time (Leah moved to Seattle from Philly in '98). I stayed with them for a month before I began living with a close friend named Daisy in a studio apartment for a total of four months during the fall/winter of 2000.

While living in the studio, I met a friend of Daisy's named Sean who was very funny, charming and cute. He and I hung out one night drinking Guinness and ended up kissing- I'm not sure if it happened that same night or not. We eventually had sex and were monogamous, but had no label. He loved me very much and respected me for my spirit and enthusiasm towards life. He's a writer as well, so we had terrific conversations and emails.

The thing with Sean though, was that he was a bit grimy for my tastes. He enjoyed filth. His place was organized enough, but not very clean. I could say the same for his body. I mean, I know he showered regularly, but his clothes....some had a smell to them that wasn't repugnant, but definitely musty, as if they were sitting in a hamper for a day or three even when clean. It was obvious that this was him and he loved himself just as he was, which I loved, but was not attracted to as he was, therefore, that was the end of my sexual relationship with Sean.

Living with Daisy worked out well, until the end. She was being extremely selfish (later she explained that she was standing up for herself) and I moved out overnight because I did not agree with her behavior towards Dean whom I felt had been nothing less than generous and kind with both of us. I went back to Juliet and Leah's place for a couple of weeks, then moved to Philly immediately afterwards. By the end of that month (and year), on New Year's Day of 2001, I moved to Manhattan, where Babs lived.

Babs is from Seattle and had moved to Manhattan when I left for Argentina. I used to detest the idea of living in NYC and say, "You couldn't pay me to live there!" I felt ready to go there and spread my feelings of love, for that's what I felt I was born on earth to do (what the 'shrooming experience helped me realize). What better place to be than Manhattan?

It was worlds better than I'd imagined. I fell in love with Manhattan in ways I never thought I would. I lived there a little less than 3 months with Babs. She had changed 180 degrees on the inside as well as the outside since I last saw her. She was anorexic and bulimic for a while. She had lost 60-80 pounds since she moved. It was difficult to see her that way, but she was happier in ways too. She knew that she had a problem and was doing her best to rectify it.

She was paying $1500/mo for a small, one bedroom apartment with no doors- not even to the bathroom. Babs had a small dog that she spoiled and adored. He was challenging for me at times, but I was happy just to be there. I got a job right away at an environmentally friendly retail store, but I couldn't stand being on my feet for 8 hours a day. I quit after 10 days. I lived there for two months before returning to Philly. I did my best to make it in Manhattan on my terms, but it's a cold world in New York City without much money for rent.

Maxine had moved to Harlem. Things were going much better between us. Raphael was in Miami by then and we were on better terms too. He called me that previous fall to tell me that he had moved to Miami with plans to stay in the U.S. until his paperwork finished processing. We still had no idea how long that would take. Moving around so much really didn't help our situation. He didn't want to hear about Joshua. I knew then that he'd never truthfully be okay with my lifestyle. He's simply not as open as I am. I wasn't too surprised.

Philadelphia was supposedly the fastest place for immigrant papers to process in the United States, so I did my best to stay in Philadelphia. I considered going back to school (possibly Temple University) to study dance. During this time is when I wrote my very first song ("Playing"). I wrote it just to see if I could. I sang it to Paula. I don't recall what she said about it, if anything. It made me very happy to do for it always seemed like such a difficult thing to me. Mom bought me a pair of beautiful speakers for Christmas in '99. I barely used them because I moved around so often. They were too big to take with me. I loved them and was anxious to settle into my new place, wherever that was so I could put them to good use.

Raphael visited Philadelphia twice that spring. That is when he met my mom for the first time, my brother, my grandmother and other members of my family. He stayed at my mom's the first time. For his second visit I got a hotel. A friend of mine said that she could hook us up with a discount. It gave us freedom and privacy, for he surprised me with how much better he was as a lover. He had moved to Miami because he knew a lot of people there. He thought about moving to Philadelphia, but we both really wanted to live in New York. However, once I looked into attending school for dance, I was set on the University of Washington. So I returned to Seattle for the fourth time in mid-July, 2001.

In the beginning of July, I almost took an apartment in Philly, Bill's place in downtown Philly. He was moving. It was big, cheap and conveniently located, but I was more into the idea of attending school in Seattle and that's when Leah told me about someone she knew who was moving out of her apartment in Capitol Hill. The rent was only $650 for a big one-bedroom apartment, within walking distance of downtown and tons of stores. I was financially strapped due to a misunderstanding with the hotel Raphael and I stayed at for our anniversary weekend (very nice), but I managed to get my plane ticket and move to Seattle anyway.

I started working almost immediately upon my return as a ticket agent in the heart of downtown Seattle. I quit the second day, but the owner was so freaked out about me leaving that I agreed to stay for a couple of weeks until he found a suitable replacement. I was good at the job, but I did not like how high strung the owner was or the throngs of people who came most days to purchase tickets and ask for local information.

The owner's business was operated out of an information booth at a major tourist attraction. ALL types of people approached me on a daily basis. After a while, I didn't think the job was THAT bad. The owner was the worst. He had drastic mood swings and tended to blow things way out of proportion (drama queen). His employees never knew when this would happen. Never knowing how he'd react to something made me feel like I was constantly walking on eggshells. I kept the job because he worked at a different location and we mainly communicated

via telephone. It was also nice because it paid $10/hr, I got free
tickets to shows for me and friends and it was within walking distance of
my place.

My rent was too much though on top of bills. I wasn't making
enough money at the ticket place and, as I made clear, I didn't like the
owner, so I began to steal from him, with the intention of paying him
back- eventually. I never intended to steal close to $1000! I would have
never stolen a thing from him had I not disliked him so much. Some
days I'd take $40-$60 and treat myself to dinner just because he pissed
me off so badly. I took on a second job sometime that fall ('01) making
photocopies of legal documents during the graveyard shift. That lasted
about 6 weeks. If I didn't have to stand on my feet the entire 8-hour shift
while there, I would've quit the ticketing job.

On the morning of September 11, 2001, my phone rang twice
within 15 minutes around 6:30am. People don't usually call my place
that early, ever, so when I woke up, I checked my messages right away.
My mom called me first with news about the twin towers. I turned on
the television and saw what had happened. Even though Babs had
stopped talking to me by then (I was too "hippie-ish" for her), I called
her right away to make sure that she was okay, which she thankfully
was.

Babs' place in Soho was only a 15-minute walk away from the
towers. It's how we easily found our way home ("just walk towards the
towers"). It was crazy to me that they were now gone. I wasn't surprised
we were attacked though, for I'd learned over the years (in politically
aware Seattle) that our government has done countless terrible and vile
things all over the world. How could we truly expect to bully everybody
else and not feel the repercussions of our actions? Somebody was bound
to retaliate at some point. I feel for all hurt and lives damaged by all acts
of violence and anger.

During this time I met a man named Nathan. He worked at a
fancy restaurant across the street from my ticket booth. I wasn't nearly
as taken with him as I was with Joshua, but there was something about
him that caught my attention- repeatedly. We kept seeing each other
because the somewhat private bathroom that I had to use was right next
to his fancy restaurant. I saw him from time to time passing by on the
stairs. One time he offered me some fresh mint leaves that he'd just
purchased from the Farmer's Market. I have a thing for mint, especially
fresh mint leaves. He had my full attention.

One night, I ate dinner there by myself while writing in my journal. He made me a salad with strawberries the he cut into the shape of hearts and placed around the plate. That did it for me. I liked him. He kept coming out of the kitchen to talk to me when he had a little time. He had the brightest, bluest eyes I'd ever seen. He asked me to wait for him to get off work so we could walk home together. His apartment was on the way to my own.

He ended up coming back to my place. He took a bath there because I had a claw foot tub (man, that tub was great!). I let him sleep in bed with me (not "the norm). I'd already talked to him here and there and we talked for hours that night. He was super nice. I hadn't had sex with anyone since Bill- one week in July, right before I moved (he and his love had broken up). I didn't have much furniture yet. He wanted to stay and I felt very relaxed and at ease with Nathan. I didn't think that anything serious was going to happen. I thought that he might initiate something, but I wasn't worried about it.

Nathan asked to kiss me before we went to sleep. I told him that I thought he was attractive, but I didn't want to kiss him because sexuality has ruined many of my possible friendships with guys. He assured me that it wouldn't ruin ours. I hesitated, but in the end, kissed him anyway. All we did was kiss that night. It was sweet and nice. I gave him a key to my place within the week because he loved it so much and I enjoyed having him there.

I was severely disappointed when I saw my apartment for the first time. It was old, not very clean and didn't have a separate wall or door to the bedroom. It was spacious and convenient, but I wouldn't have picked it for myself. I was finishing up Leah's friend's lease. I didn't have to pay a deposit or last month's rent and I moved right around the time that I wanted to move, which is why I took it.

Nathan made me appreciate my place more. His apartment was a 10-15 minute walk away from mine. He lived with his brother who was in a semi-famous punk rock band. Nathan adored his little brother, but not their place, so we spent most of our time at my place. When I came home after I first gave him my keys, he had flowers on my counter for me with a note saying he'd be back later. He frequently did sweet things like that.

He made me countless vegetarian and vegan meals from scratch. It would take him 4-8 hours to make a soup that would last me all week long. He was no longer a cook. He got a job as a carpenter. He worked on an island across the water from downtown Seattle called Bainbridge

Island. He loved cooking for me- and I loved him cooking for me. It's the first time I'd ever eaten so well on a regular basis in my life! I think of that time whenever I get lazy about cooking.

We rented movies a lot, massaged each other, shared books, thoughts and feelings. We were pretty damn open with each other, but I could sense his daily anxieties. He was great about picking up things before heading to my house. We'd stay in all night. He worked hard during the week, so our "down time" was relished. I was smoking cigarettes at that time (I started again in June), as was he, but I told him that I planned to quit soon. I told him that I didn't like kissing smokers when I didn't smoke. He wanted to quit anyway, but I questioned whether or not he really would.

I gave up smoking cigarettes on Halloween. He didn't. He said that he'd be through with them by New Year's. It wasn't even that he smoked that much. I just knew how unhealthy he was overall. He didn't really care about how he treated his body. He ate junk food consistently, drank alcohol 4-5 times a week, smoked at least 3-5 cigarettes on a daily basis and I don't even know how much coffee he drank. It was normal to drink obscene amounts in Seattle. His sleeping habits were horrible too. Yes, my lifestyle had been worse than his at times, but at that time, it was not. I was very healthy and worked hard at becoming more health conscious. He was not helping in this regard and I was concerned about becoming too romantically invested in him.

By December, I cared for him a great deal. I attempted to create space between us a few times, but he kept asking me to give him another chance. I was doing my best to stay focused and live positively. I even told the owner of the ticket place (I stole money from Sept- Nov, give or take) that I stole $1000 from him. I was reading "Conversations with God- Book 1" and I'd read that lying is lying still when you keep something important from someone that you know they would rather know. I agreed.

I sent the owner an email explaining everything and outlined a plan to pay him back all the money I took, even though I had no money at the time. He was SHOCKED, but he didn't fire me (probably to make sure he got his money). He asked me to give him $100 out of every paycheck (every 2 weeks) until I paid him back, which I did over the next 4-5 months.

Those were some TOUGH times. First off, let me mention again how much I ABHOR cold weather, particularly an entire SEASON of it! It really doesn't rain as much as people think it does in Seattle. It's just cold, overcast and drizzling half of fall, all winter and half of spring. It pretty much stays in the 40s-60s, but it's awful to me (the temperature, not the beauty). I did NOT have a problem with the humidity and heat of the east coast!

Where I worked, in the booth, there was an open window in front of me at all times, so I was always exposed to outside temperatures. I had a heater AND a heating pad, gloves, scarf, hat, jacket, the works! There were no nice views where I lived or worked. It affected me severely because I knew how many GORGEOUS vistas Seattle has all over. There were lots of homeless people and druggies all around that part of the city- where I lived and where I worked. It took me 20-30 minutes to walk to work, which was a nice and pretty walk. With the sun setting around 4pm at the height of winter though, it really got depressing at times. I don't enjoy being depressed (some do). I'm extremely strong-willed, so I worked EXTRA HARD at attaining and maintaining a loving and positive outlook on the world. I knew that the sun still beamed beyond the clouds, even when I couldn't see it.

Nathan began pulling away in mid-December. I could tell that something was up, but I was too fixated on my own life, with Christmas coming and all. It was the VERY first year I got something (simple) for every single person in my humongous family (7 aunts and uncles and TONS of cousins) and everyone that I could think of, including friends. It was quite an ordeal buying them a month ahead of time, wrapping them and shipping them all in time while working and spending time with friends and a boyfriend.

Right after Christmas, Nathan came to my house one night to get something. I got out of bed to ask him what was up. All of a sudden, he broke down and told me that he was high on heroin and cocaine. He showed me how to tell if he was high by looking at his pupils. In dim light, his pupils looked like pinpoints. Normally, they'd be more dilated (open, to let more light in). It was weird. I had friends who'd done LOTS of various drugs and a few had even tried heroin, but I had never known an addict and here my boyfriend was my first encounter. He'd been using off and on for 6 or 7 years. He told me that he was using it to maintain for a while, shooting up every other week or so, but recently it had gotten out of hand and he wanted me to help him kick.

To say that I was surprised was an understatement. I could hardly believe any of it. Here I was, again, in another fucked up romance. How??? BECAUSE I DIDN'T TAKE ENOUGH TIME TO REALLY GET TO KNOW THIS PERSON! (How many times does it take?) I was in love with him and I was in love with love. I decided to stand by him and help him as best I could.

There's a pill that addicts can take that will block any opiate from getting them high. The danger is of them overdosing just to get high, which no amount will do. No opiate will get them high with the "blocker" in place. He knew about this pill and asked me to go to the doctor with him to get it. I was designated by Nathan to be the person to watch him take this pill every day, which was mandatory in order to get a prescription. There was no one else he would ask. His brother knew that he used to use, but he never told his brother how serious his problem had become again.

I got up at 6 am almost every day (and I am so NOT a morning person) to meet him at a coffee shop or some place to watch him take this pill. He wouldn't let me meet him every day though. How could I force him? It was his decision. It took 3 days for the pill to wear off for him to get high again, or else he'd get really sick. He did use during this time and dealt with the sickness. I knew and prayed each time that he would stick with it. I would constantly wonder if I would get a phone call from his brother or co-worker telling me that he was dead. I could tell how painful it all was for him. We stopped being sexually intimate almost immediately after he told me about his use. It's not even something I enforced. It just happened. He felt ashamed and I honestly feel that once he told me, he became okay with heroin being his one and only "love".

One of the toughest things during that time was that I didn't even have a chance to grieve over the loss of our romantic relationship. Sometimes I felt jealous of heroin's effects on him. How did it have such a hold of him? It was hard to understand. I didn't even have his friendship- not in the ways I look for in real friends. It was one of the hardest experiences with another person I have EVER gone through.

He lied to me a few times (that I knew of) about those pills. He'd made up reasons he couldn't meet me and say that he took it. Sometimes he wouldn't call me for a few days. Every day I didn't hear from him felt like an eternity and where I worked was right across the street from where a lot of people bought and used heroin. I often wondered if he was around, high, looking at me. One day he told me that indeed he had been looking at me from across the street and I never saw him.

One night, I was on the phone with him and he told me that he didn't have any money to catch the ferry the next morning to go to work (this is the same guy who paid for a month of my rent just so I wouldn't move out). I told him I'd meet him in the morning and give him the fare. I went to his place (I had a key) and went to the bathroom before waking him up. Somewhere around the toilet, I saw a needle half full of brown shit (heroin) and in the back of the toilet (the lid was off) were at least a few empty needles sitting in the water. I squirted out the heroin into the toilet and then I woke him up. I told him what I'd done and he got pissed! He freaked out about needing it to get through work. He was not the person I'd met several months prior. He never hit me , screamed at me or hurt me, but I hated watching what he allowed this drug to do to him.

I had picked up another job a month or so before this incident, so I was waking up at 5 am, at work by 6 am and worked all day until 6:30 or 7 pm WHILE doing EVERYTHING I could think of to help this man that I loved kick heroin. It was all so sad and depressing, but I really worked on taking care of myself as best I could, day by day. I started doing yoga every morning just to keep me centered and feeling some sort of peace inside. It was the only thing that calmed and anchored me, that allowed me to hold on to my sense of "things will get better" throughout the emotional turmoil that was my life.

The last straw was when my mom came into town (March 2002). She and my oldest nephew visited for 10 days. They took the bus for 3 days from Philly (mom's afraid to fly). The day before they arrived, I shopped for Nathan because he didn't want to leave the house. He was afraid that if he left his house that day, he'd use, so I told him I'd get everything he needed, including movies, to stay inside for the day. I was almost late to work running to get him a pack of cigarettes.

When I called him from work the very next day, the day my mom got into town (she took a cab to my place and waited for me to finish working), I was right up the street from where he lived. I asked him how he was doing. He asked me to pick him up some medicine to stop diarrhea. I picked it up and headed to his place to drop off his medicine BEFORE seeing my own family, after they were on a bus for three days. When I got to his place he told me that he had lied to me the day before. He used and was sick because he took one of those pills too soon. I was done. He lied to me AGAIN! It made me feel so powerless and infuriated. I wished so badly that I could kick his habit for him.

I really did try not to take it all so personally, but it was too hard. I felt broken and defeated. I cried and emotionally gave up. I was devastated. For 3 months I had given and given, believing that at some point he'd stop. How could he not with my help? I knew that I couldn't keep it up, but part of me wanted to. I wanted to love him unconditionally and have enduring faith in him. I did, and still do, but I had to step back and change the ways I expressed my love for Nathan and for myself. I didn't understand why he couldn't just stop. I knew it was hard, but other people did it.

Nathan asked me not to give up on him, to help him one more time That wasn't the first time he'd asked "one more time." It was getting harder and harder to have real faith. At first I agreed, but then I changed my mind. I'd heard it all before. I refused to set myself up again. I was drained. I didn't have it in me to truly believe him one more time. I went home. My mom knew about Nathan's addiction. It was such a part of my life at that point; there was no keeping it from her. The next day, he called and we talked for over 3 hours. He kept saying how much he wished heroin didn't exist. I felt like I was repeating myself over and over. We were going nowhere. I told him that I was taking a break from him, for the sake of myself.

I was in a weak place in my life already and Nathan really was not helping. I didn't feel like I could hold us up any longer by myself and I didn't want to go down with him. He did look out for me in the sense that he made me promise him that I'd never try heroin or oxycontin. The former was never even a consideration, but the latter, was going around my circle of friends. I was tempted, just to see what heroin's effects were like (they're derived from the same opiate), but I'm not a pill popper. I never did it. I wouldn't. I still think it was sweet of him to show concern. He was one of the sweetest guys I'd ever been with. He treated himself terribly, but he treated me like gold, at least, for the first half of our relationship.

My mom and nephew had a messed up trip because it was so cold that spring. It snowed the first day of spring that year! They had already left by then. We stayed in watching movies a lot. It was tough because of the schedule I was working. I couldn't afford to take that many days off. I had no privacy in my apartment due to the lack of doors. I SLOWLY re-cooperated from the chaos in my life. I quit my second job (I had to touch and scrape too many cold things). I continued practicing yoga on a daily basis and I focused on my plans for that summer. I didn't know what they were, just something different. It had to be better than that reality.

One day, about a month later (April '02), I was with a friend of mine named Yuki who had come to meet me after work and we went to use the bathroom across the street, the one next to Nathan's old job.

Yuki told me that he thought he saw someone shooting up in the bathroom. I knew it might be my paranoia, but I got this weird feeling that it might be Nathan. I hoped it wasn't.

I waited to see the guy come out of the bathroom. It was Nathan. It was the first time I'd seen him since the day I left his apartment when my mom arrived. I watched, as his pupils got smaller right in front of me. We were talking about his brother getting married and bullshit. I just wanted to cry. He was obviously uncomfortable. I still wished I could do something to stop him from using, but what more could I do that I hadn't done already? I wasn't ready to be around him more or even talk, not yet.

My master plan for the summer was to go to Philly (I'd been postponing a visit for months), work and save money there during the summer, then move to Los Angeles in the fall. I placed an ad in the local newspaper of the area where I wished to live in Philadelphia (Mt. Airy and Chestnut Hill). I was looking for a place to stay in exchange for light housekeeping or low rent.

A man answered my ad that sounded like a perfect match! He was planning on being away frequently on business. He had a vacation planned for the whole month of August and wanted someone to watch his house while he was gone. He invited me to stay with him as early as mid-June through the end of August. He had 3 kids who stayed at their mom's most of the time. They spent their summers in Michigan, so I'd have the house pretty much to myself.

Bill visited Seattle for the first time in May, right before I left for Philly. He stayed at my place for the first week and our friend Derek's place (Derek is Juliet's younger brother who had moved to Seattle the year before and had played music with Bill in Philly before moving) the second week he was there. We had a blast! Bill decided to move to Seattle. I think part of the reason was Ariana's sister, Alannah. Bill and Alannah took a strong liking to one another upon first sight. I had a feeling that they would. I'd told them both about each other. Right after they met, they each asked me separately, "Who's that again??"

Bill and I were in Philly at the same time for a few weeks after his return. He was most excited about his move to Seattle because he's a bass player and Derek's a drummer (Alannah was leaving soon to travel, so she wouldn't be in Seattle much longer). Derek, Bill, Juliet and I all went to Central High School together (different grades). I knew Derek because of Juliet. The last time I was in Philly (mid-March through mid-July) Derek and I became friends on our own, apart from Juliet. We hung out in Seattle here and there. We didn't have the same group of friends and different lifestyles, but it was always great to hang out when we did. We're like family to one another.

Bill was excited to spend what time he could with Alannah. From the first day they met, he was struck. It was funny. I knew Bill would dig Alannah, but I had no idea just how much. Alannah's a painter and world traveler. She already had plans to leave in August for England. Bill wanted to spend more time with her before she left. When he went back to Seattle, they became lovers. It was a whirlwind for them both and then she left.

Shortly after I returned to Philadelphia, I visited Devon in North Carolina for a week during the month of June. I wondered if anything would happen between us. Nothing did that time, nor has it happened any other time since we broke up (aside from that one time two months later). We got into a fight during my visit. I love him dearly as a friend. Being there made me remember all of the reasons we're not together anymore. It was the first time I'd seen him in a long time. I was looking good too. Practicing yoga (cooking at home and eating well) since February got me in excellent shape. It was the first time in my life I felt completely comfortable in a bikini. It was a good vacation (other than the fight), a nice break from the norm. I LOVED how hot it was!!

After being in Seattle so long, I was ready for the east coast heat- and I got it! I went biking in 98-degree weather. The 3 H's prevailed all summer long: Hazy, Hot and Humid! My plan to work and save wasn't going as planned though. I couldn't find a decent job, mainly because I wasn't willing to commit to a place for more than 6 months. I still wanted to move to L.A. in the fall. My funds were quickly dwindling and I began to worry, in my beautiful 5-bedroom home that belonged to the man whose house I looked after. What to do?

An old co-worker and supervisor that I used to talk to in another location at my ticketing job was online almost every day. The house had a computer that I could freely use, so I got on chat to keep in touch. None of us liked the ticket company owner. The supervisor, Susan, kept saying that she wished I were there to help her because they were so swamped. She asked me a few times to go back and work for her. One day I finally took her up on her offer. I really didn't want to work with my old boss again, but he was hardly EVER at their location, it was easy work, with people I liked, making decent money. I wasn't sure he'd even hire me back, but I was a great worker. Sure enough, he did rehire me.

A big factor in moving to Seattle for the FIFTH (and possibly final) time was hearing Bill and Derek tell me that they were performing at a bar/restaurant in my old neighborhood at the end of August. It was a small performance just to attract some people in a new place. I was excited about it though, for the experience of singing with Bill and Derek before I left them in Seattle was like no other.

I had never sung like I had with them that day in the garage before I left for Philly. We played "Where did our love go?" (all FUNKtified) and it rocked through my whole soul. I felt alive in ways I had never even imagined (and I was getting over being sick!). I thought Bill, Derek and I had a lot of potential and I wanted to see what we could do. I'm all about giving my best to my dreams so that I don't regret what "could've been".

I used the very last of my money to buy my plane ticket to Seattle. I left three days after I decided to move back. I worked the very next day. I was working on music every day preparing for this show with the boys in two weeks. One of my co-workers named Tonjia played a tape for me of her music one day while we were driving around. I loved it so much that later I made her play it for the boys. They were impressed and wanted to use her in the show as well.

It moved me. I loved Tonjia's music. She wrote her own songs, played the guitar and sang. I had no idea she was so talented! That was the case with many of my friends, which I was just beginning to realize. She makes movies too. Ariana writes books, plays, and screenplays. Nowadays she plays guitar and sings as well. Amber, another co-worker at the ticketing place is a gifted writer and orator, yet has hardly had any training in either. Many of my friends are naturally creative in some way or another. They're so inspiring. We all feed off of each other.

The whole process of putting the show together and performing was stressful for all of us, especially since it was the first time any of us were involved in a real show. I sang a few songs ("Playing", "Truths in Disguise", which I wrote within those 2 weeks and a couple of covers). There were 3 or 4 other vocalists who sang and played guitar during the show as well. Derek and Bill accompanied us all. They loved it. I thought the show went well overall, but I was not happy with the attitudes when it came to practice. I didn't like depending on other people to show up relatively on time or to concentrate on the songs we were working on. It was like being in a romantic relationship with a bunch of people. That is when I first thought about being a solo artist.

Not having my own place, no money, working a lot and feeling stretched thin were wearing on me. I was staying at Dean's, once again.

Juliet, Derek, Bill, and a friend of Juliet's named Cathy (singer and guitarist too) all lived together in a house with a garage (right down the street from my last apartment). Juliet and I hadn't talked for a few years. She had a hard time being honest and open with me and at a certain point, I wouldn't put up with it anymore. I didn't like tiptoeing around her or trying to decode what she was really saying.

Juliet hated me for calling her out on certain feelings of anger (or whatever she was "hiding"). She'd try to suppress them. The fact was, whether she acknowledged it or not, I could feel whatever she was feeling, which sucked, but to blatantly act like those feelings weren't there was too hard for me, especially as one of her best friends. If it was an occasional thing, fine, but this was too constant. I wished to at least acknowledge them and move on. Once I brought things to the forefront and expressed that I didn't care to return to "ignorance land", she stopped talking to me altogether.

That was about 3 years prior to this time. That's why I lived with Dean again, or else I would've stayed with them. Dean had more space anyway and lived close-by everything as well. He loved having me around too. He's almost 25 years older than me and has treated me as well as he would his own daughter- consistently- throughout the years ever since I met him. He's down to earth. He does lie a lot, but rarely about anything important anyway. He tries to make everyone happy and he's very self-conscious. He's always looked out for me and has done his best to do whatever he can to help me.

Dean is an alcoholic too though. Throughout most of our friendship, he's been sober, however, during this period, he had a relapse. He was out of control. It was simply more difficult to be around him. I just wanted some peace and quiet. He talked a whole lot and people frequently stopped by his apartment because he was the manager. I moved in with a friend of his whom I knew used to be a junkie (heroin addict). He'd known her to steal from him, but supposedly she'd cleaned up her act and had her shit together.

O yeah! Brief side note, speaking of heroin addicts, I saw Nathan TWICE within two weeks of my return to Seattle. It was so strange because we never ran into each other, even when we lived 10-15 minutes apart. It was so hard seeing him. The first time was driving by him while I was in Tonjia's car. The second time, he was walking on the opposite side of the street. I went up to him and hugged him, but it was so fake. He was not happy to see me. He didn't look good. His pupils were tiny. I knew he was high. He was totally uncomfortable, so I let him go- again.

Dean had a friend named Stephanie who was a heroin addict. She said that she didn't use that much. She was on methadone and had fibromyalgia. Her father and brother had sexually abused her, repeatedly, when she was younger and her mother always denied it. She was a very pretty woman with a very messed up life. She was an alcoholic as well and a tough cookie! I felt for her. She was constantly escaping pain of some sort or another.

I didn't have enough money to get my own place any time soon. Stephanie didn't work, so she was home often and smoked cigarettes inside of her apartment. We shared her large studio. There was nowhere for me to go in her place, except the bathroom, for any time alone or privacy, which I crave normally, but especially when I'm heavily stressed. Stephanie went away for a week and asked me to watch her cat, which was heaven! I knew I had to find my own place SOON after I came home one day and she and a friend had just shot up. I could feel the difference in the air as soon as I walked in. I felt like I went into another dimension or something. Her friend ran to the bathroom to puke within minutes of my arrival.

I was done with Capitol Hill and downtown Seattle. I had always lived in that area of Seattle. I yearned for the water (there's water all around Seattle. It's a peninsula), mountains (2 mountain ranges and Mt. Rainier), and sky (there are MANY spectacular views of the sky all over the city). Amber lived in west Seattle and loved that area, as did I. The apartments were more than I could afford at the time, but I knew that if I waited long enough, I'd find something that I could afford that had at least one of the aforementioned things I desperately longed for.

I searched and searched, until I found a place right in my price range with the most BREATHTAKING view of the water, sky, and mountains. I still shake my head in awe just thinking about it. It's quiet and beautiful and I'm quite content to stay here another year. It's where I now live. I moved in the beginning of October '02. After Stephanie's, I stayed at Tonjia's while she was in Korea visiting family. I watched Tonjia's 3 cats while she was gone. It all worked out perfectly. It's kind of eerie.

After my home life transformed into such a wondrous place, my work life went down the drain. When Tonjia left for Korea, Susan (our supervisor) was a ROYAL pain in the ass!! I seriously wanted to cry a few times. I did cry at least once from her yelling at me or giving me a hard time. She was mean, rude and under tremendous stress from the owner. It didn't stop when Tonjia returned (Tonjia was her assistant). She was out of line with customers, clients and co-workers/friends, like Amber and Tonjia whom I really care about. Her hypocrisy and tyrannical attitude drove me mad! It was an unhealthy environment that I refused to stay in any longer. So I quit and encouraged my friends to do the same as soon as they could, for it was a miserable and wretched environment for anyone.

I gave my notice and worked right up until the last day. Susan called me in to work another day (it took all my might to stay as long as I did. It was November 9th, the day before my birthday). I worked the day that she asked. She reminded me of all the reasons I couldn't take being there (it wasn't ALWAYS terrible). She asked me to work one more day at a later date, but by mid-afternoon I never, EVER planned to go back. A few days later, I sent her an email stating all the reasons why I will never work for that company again. At one point I thought perhaps we could still be friends. Susan was not a friend I cared to have.

That was almost 3 weeks ago. I've been looking for a new job and my passions lie in music, books, movies, television and art. I've been focusing more on those things, which is how this zine came about. I love to film all types of things with my camcorder, particularly me pleasuring myself with music (sensually! not graphically). I AM a woman. We tend to be more into foreplay, seduction and sensuality. I've been able to have orgasms on cue with the climactic parts of songs for over 11 years now. I've gotten pretty damn good! At one point I was going to sell copies of my footage, but it's not the route I'd like to take with my art right now. MAYBE later.

I recorded my two songs with the help of my friend Mike. I sang. He did all the rest of the work, including live drums. Singing moves me in ways that nothing else does. I don't like the idea of constantly touring, but I do like the idea of getting paid to travel and sing, even if it's only a fraction of what big name artists get. I dream of doing something I love as much as I do singing. I feel like I'm channeling love when I sing. I once (and only once) dreamt that I was a song. I saw nothing. I WAS each word being sung. I had the dream in Argentina. The song was "I'll be there for you" by Bon Jovi. I recorded "Wanted Dead or Alive" (a classic) in Mike's studio (garage and computer) and it came out super cool (dual a'cappella tracks with vocal reflection).

A year ago, in February, while I was helping Nathan kick, I

divorced Raphael. We had a falling out over our views on death. It came up in relation to the death of his grandfather. We had an INS interview coming up in Miami. That's where his paperwork was or going to at that point for he knew that he was going to stay there and I wasn't settled in any city. I did not want to move to Miami though. He didn't want to move to Seattle (this was right after I moved to Seattle the fourth time).

Raphael was really upset that he wasn't in Argentina when his grandfather died. He knew how close to death he was, for he told me while I was there. He knew that he couldn't leave Miami on a moment's notice once he had arrived there. I felt that if not being with his grandfather when he died was a risk he didn't want to take, it would've been better for him to stay until he passed. I was as compassionate as I could be for weeks, possibly months with him, but I was going through a great deal of stress myself and couldn't take his selfishness or close mindedness anymore. Our relationship had been too imbalanced for too long. I was done. I divorced him so that we could possibly be friends again and in order for our marriage not to create logistical problems in our lives in relation to the government paperwork.

I've talked to him once since then, back in June of this past year. He sounded weird on the phone. He's remarried now. He told me that it's "for real". I took that to mean that he didn't take my feelings and our marriage as seriously as I did. I believe that he did really love me, but we weren't the most compatible romantically for each other at that time. In superficial ways we are, but not in fundamental, value based ways. That took time to figure out (There's LESSON #1 AGAIN!).

In no way do I regret marrying Raphael. He taught me many, many things that I'll never forget. From the pleasures and natural highs I felt just being around him to the spiritual insights I gained through our experiences on through the pain associated with the disappointments of unfulfilled expectations and sudden change. Wherever he is, I hope that he's happy. I wish that for everyone.

My life might seem crazy, but whose life isn't? I'd like to help as many people as I possibly can with honesty, openness and love. That's why I'm sharing all that I am- even down to using my real name (almost all other names have been changed for privacy).

I made one last attempt to see Joshua a couple of months ago. He said that he'd call the cops on me if I contacted him again. I had called his job (he had his own furniture business) and asked about ordering a chair. I wondered if he'd deliver it. I didn't want to freak him out if he was the delivery guy (I don't think he had any employees. It was a web based vintage furniture business). I could've just let him show up and see me, but I didn't want it to happen that way.

Once I told him (via email) that it was me, he threatened to call the cops if I didn't leave him alone. I didn't think anything I'd done warranted that extreme of a reaction. He OBVIOUSLY wants nothing to do with me anymore. He's moving to California anyway (says so on the website). It's difficult to let go of him because of how much pleasure he brought into my life from that one month alone. I use that inspiration still to this day. I wish him all the best too and once again, let go.

Letting go can be such a chore for me. Patience is another, but I am learning. There is no substitute for good, ol' fashioned practice!

Practice! Practice! Practice!

A few more things to know about me:

-I don't ever plan to bear any children. I MIGHT adopt in my 40's or 50's. My brother has 3 children that he has a tough enough time supporting. The world has enough people. I LOVE children, but I feel I do best as a "fill-in" mom.

-I didn't get into how much I love to travel. I'll do it for the rest of my life. Warm, beautiful places are at the top of my list.

-In case it's not obvious by now, I don't "date". I'm a HUGE proponent for self-love. I haven't been sexually involved with anyone since Nathan (a year ago). I intend to take things SLOW with anyone I'm attracted to, for we/love are all we need.

May we all consciously grow, change, and love more and more each day.

This is a poem (now a song titled "Any Day Now") that I wrote on Valentine's Day, 2001 using Joshua as my muse:

Whose fault is it anyway-
Yours for having such breathtaking beauty or mine
For recognizing it?

I'll take the blame
Whatever is the game
Because Love is my name
And I shall remain
In time stood still
With a soul left to fill
That claims not to kill
The spirit of goodwill.
Looking straight into your heart
From the very early start
I could tell that you were smart
So I let you play your part.

Just continue on my friend
I'm sure we'll meet again
Until that day I'll spend
Moments without end
Thinking of this story
Of times desultory
Disguised as purgatory
With you in shining glory.
And every day I pray
True love will find a way
Into your heart some day
To kiss me as I lay
Dreaming of you
Is all I can do
To remember what's true
While I'm here passing through
Time and space
This capricious place
Where I see your face

In exquisite grace

Not a second goes by
That I choose to deny
Copious reasons why
It's prodigious to cry
Out these feelings you produce
I exhort, they are of use
To transcend abject abuse
So I keep you as my muse.

"Playing"- The song I wrote while living at mom's to see if I could do it:

Show me what to do.
Tell me what to say.
I am lost in you.
Help me find my way.

I go to sleep to never wake,
unsure how to undertake
this task of being me-
unashamedly crazy.

(chorus)
Here in the middle of this world...
Just playing in the middle of this world.
Come here to the middle of this world.
No fear in the middle of this world.

Go ahead capitulate.
I'm here to communicate
with ears to understand
these fears of a promised land.

This pulse reaches deep inside
never on a better ride
replete and full of pride
because I don't care to hide.

Not here in the middle of this world.
Just playing in the middle of this world.
Come here to the middle of this world.
No fear in the middle of this world.

Touch me.
Hold me.
Release me.
Know me.

I said-
Just touch me...
Hold me...
Release me...
Know me.

So sublime
thinking 'bout you all the time
no fear of losing my mind,
not afraid to shine
and show how we're all intertwined

Right here in the middle of this world
Just playing in the middle of this world
Come here to the middle of this world.
Stay here in the middle of this world.

"Truths in Disguise"- was written for the show with Derek and Bill
when I first returned to Seattle this last time in order for us to have more
original material. Some emotions in regards to Nathan are expressed
here as if I were he, an addict. I'm addicted to love! ;P

When the sun comes up
and the new day begins,
I wish I were filled with hope
and forgot the fact that things end.
Could it be possible
that life is never-ending?
Please don't show me where
there is harm in believing.

(chorus)
Now don't criticize
until you are wise,
to the many lies
that are truths in disguise.

Listening to music...
dancing...floating....
I can't refuse it
feeding and hoping
our souls open up to this
allowing us to be imbued
with this world's most precious gifts
mere words simply won't do.

(chorus)

[Drums and bass only]

These fantasies
are the keys
to opening our hearts
in ways we can only dream...
don't wake me...
just let me be
so carefree
endlessly
with eyes wide
seeing all
I can see....
don't wake me....

oooooooooohhhhhhho

na na... na na... na na....

Sunday, May 28, 2006   Philadelphia, Pa
2:41am

    Hello, again, curious reader! How many things have changed- and some have stayed the same- since I started my autobiographical pages in 2002. It's been about a year since I've touched this book. I have written out the first 26 years of my life twice. The zine that I published was written by hand. I published it that way too, like in the beginning of "Illusions".

    When I decided to turn the zine into a book, I had to type it into a computer, which I did a year and a half ago (It was 67 pages then). I've gone back over it since then to edit. I will go back at least once more to elaborate on certain themes and interests that I feel are important to mention that I might have forgotten to include.

    Now, I would like to bring this book up to date, to where I am these days. Three and a half years ago is where my zine ended. Now it will be a book. It's incredible to think of all that has transpired during that time as well as who I was then, in contrast to who I am now.

    Who am I now?

Let's find out…

Chapter 3
Back to The Emerald City

I was unemployed for about 6-7 weeks during the winter of '02-'03. I self published 67 pages of my life that I had written by hand in less than 12 hours. My good friend Amber has a wonderful dad who helped me by letting me use his single sheet copier at his small insurance office. It took MANY HOURS to make around 15-20 copies, but I did it. I looked up all of the places (mainly bookstores) that I thought would carry zines and called them to see if they'd carry mine and what I was to do from there.

Within the next few days, I made my rounds and 7 stores carried my zine. This was right after the New Year. I was doing my best not to panic about rent and bills and praying for unemployment to come through for me from the ticketing place. It was worth a shot. It didn't happen. The unemployment rate was high in Seattle during that time. I was living in a naturally beautiful area in a cabin-like house one vertical block (BIG hill) from the beach. I loved being home to watch the sunset behind the Olympic mountain range with the water of the Puget Sound mirroring it's astounding beauty. I finally had both of my speakers in Seattle with me. I played my music and zoned out on nature while staring out my bedroom windows stretching, dancing, talking on the phone and/or smoking some of the northwest's finest.

When I first moved into that house on Alki, 2 people were living there- mother and daughter- and they were looking for 3 roommates because the daughter was leaving soon. The first room I moved into was enormous. It was the most expensive room because of it's size and it had it's own bathroom. It was closest to the kitchen too, which was nice. The place had a washer and a dryer as well. I paid $550 a month plus one-fourth of the utilities.

This guy named Kyle moved out of the front room right before New Years and I took his room. He was a cool guy. Kyle was the first lover of Coldplay I'd ever known. He made me want to hear them, but it still took a couple of years for me to fall in love. He was black, he was gay and the mom roommate was not feeling either of those things, which was why he was moving out after only being there for less than 3 months. Alki was also far from a lot of things and Kyle didn't have a car. He was a student who went to school on Capitol Hill and worked downtown. I would have rather she moved.

If I could've afforded to move any place even remotely comparable, I would've. Once Kyle moved out though, my rent was even cheaper because his room cost less by it being smaller. The view was PHENOMENAL- 180 degrees of natural beauty. It had a side door that opened to the porch. We all spent many nights staring out at the water, mountains and skies of west Seattle. The sunsets were spectacles of beauty only nature could craft. I reveled in its majesty as much as possible and oftentimes gave credit where credit was due. I'd never been around such natural wonderment on a regular basis. That's why I stayed in that house.

The mom roommate was a lot to handle because she was home almost all day and liked to talk, however, she got herself in trouble with me one day when she referred to these "nigger girls" bulldozing "little ol' her" as she was coming out of a convenient store. I'm a small woman oftentimes and even when I feel "bulldozed" by people, I don't feel the need to insult them to that degree, especially in a simple story. I'd grown so accustomed to my non-racist and relatively nice friends and liberal neighborhoods that I forgot that people like her are for real and exist in the world with their ignorance running rampant to the point where she actually said the word "nigger", as if I was on her "side", to a biracial woman.

She learned quickly that those are not the words to use to tell me a story involving anyone of color and that the people in my family are people of color. I had told her this before, but she forgot and put her foot right in her mouth. I wasn't being mean, but clear in her tasting the filth of her own words, for those were my babies (my brother's kids or cousins) she could've been talking about. Regardless, they were just adolescent girls meaning no real harm who happened to be black. She had issues with the latter and sought ways to express that. I was not the one. After that incident we were cordial, but never friends.

There weren't many businesses along Alki Beach. Alki is the name of the road along that particular strip of restaurants, rental places and apartments that run parallel to the beach (some of it rocky, some sandy) along an edge of west Seattle. Ideally, I wanted to work some place within walking or biking distance from my house, which cut out all of downtown Seattle and a few other neighborhoods that offered better job prospects. I didn't really care how much I made. My rent was only $425/mo and I wasn't in a lot of debt. I was hoping to get hired at this smoothie and ice-cream place that barely had anyone come through, at least not in mid-January. They had a help wanted sign in the window, but they never called me back after I stopped in and left my information repeatedly.

One day I was walking with Brian, Amber's dad, by this pizza place that had a help wanted sign. I went in and asked for an application. The place was a bit more casual than I hoped it would be. If I was going to wait tables again, I at least wanted to make a lot of money, but the people were nice AND it was a 15 minute walk or 5 minute bike ride away from my place. So I filled out the application and dropped it back off as soon as I could, for I had a good feeling about the place.

That job was worth checking out in more ways than I ever imagined!! I started on January 13th. I don't think I had any money to my name. I had just found out 6 days prior that I was denied unemployment and my zine wasn't selling. Within a couple of weeks, I was averaging $15-$18/hr at this pizza place. When I was hired, the manager told me that I'd soon average $20/hr and more in the summer. It was hard to believe, especially after so much financial destitution. I began to realize the truth of his words within the first month. I was making $7/hr plus tips. We declared 8% of our tips and still made mad cash. It was the most steadily lucrative job I've ever had to date, averaging $3,000 a month after taxes.

Pegasus Pizza and Pasta on Alki, some of the best pizza many have ever had, made by Mexicans owned by a Greek. Go figure!! Most of the kitchen staff was Mexican. I enjoyed practicing my Spanish with them. They made me laugh a lot and kept the place relatively calm. At the head of the ship was a man who'd started as a dishwasher at 15 and then managed the place by 25. He was a simple man who was dedicated and effective, straight forward and organized. I appreciated this in a restaurant environment because too easily things can fall apart at the worst times. He's one of the biggest reasons that I stayed there for 9 months. It was great money for short shifts with good flexibility.

When I first started working there, I thought about the possibility of Joshua coming into Pegasus because it was a place frequented by the locals. I knew that he used to live in west Seattle with his parents, but he was supposedly moving to California. I had no idea if he was around or not, but he kept coming to mind. That wasn't new though.

About two weeks after I started, I was about to greet a table of 6 and had a feeling that he was sitting there. Without my glasses, it was hard for me to tell for sure. I didn't want to stare, so I just went on over and took their order. Yes, it was him. I was a little embarrassed because I wished that I was doing something so much cooler than serving at a pizza place after not seeing him for three years. I was happy to be at Pegasus though and wasn't going to let him make me feel bad about myself. I wished I wore make up that day. I set all anxieties aside and took everyone's order. His mom asked, "Josh, what are you having?" I was standing next to him at this point.

The most distinct memory I have of their entire time there is of his eyes looking up at me when he gave me his order. I know that he had to recognize me, but he didn't look surprised, which made me think that he had already seen me. He wasn't any particular way one way or the other. Maybe he was and I was too freaked out to notice. I did my very best to be normal. The feelings I had for him weren't the same. For one, he had something with meat (like lasagna) and a coke, which I would prefer my lover not to eat or drink, given the choice. He was cute still, but that's it, just cute, not "omigod!" gorgeous.

It was then that I truly realized that it is what the person's energetic exchange is with you that makes all the difference. Joshua treated me much differently years before and it was his treatment, the energy he poured forth onto me that had affected me so strongly. One of my co-workers knew him. She'd waited on him several times and lived in the neighborhood too. She said that when she saw him on the street a few times, he acted like he didn't recognize her. No matter what, something had changed. He no longer had this hold over me. I could still enjoy all that I received from our time together and see that I didn't miss out on much. At times I do wonder about his version of our story and what he's up to now.

Even though I planned to leave in September to move to St. John, U.S.V.I. (originally I was going to move to Brazil and then L.A.) my departure is not why I left Pegasus. I fell off of my bicycle on July 13th, 2003 on my way from Ariana's apartment to Bill's house to drop something off before work because I woke up early and had the time. Bill planned to come out to Alki later that day. I figured I'd save him the trip. It was all very serendipitous. I hardly EVER wake up early, for one. I felt like I was in a dream for about 12 hours, starting with the night before, due to many unusual events that had transpired. I fractured a small bone in my right wrist. The fiberglass cast encased my entire forearm.

My wrists and hands on both sides were extremely sore and not of much use. I'd never broken anything before. I was devastated by all of the sudden changes. Right after the accident, I could barely move my wrists any way at all. It was a slippery zigzag curb on an incline that caused my tire to catch and throw me from my bike. Using my hands to break my fall to the ground is what caused so much damage. I don't even really remember it happening.

The pain was intense and came in waves. When I realized how injured I was and that I couldn't go to work, I called the managers of Pegasus right away. It was early in the morning, so they were still asleep. It was then that I started to cry. I cried and cried and cried some more. It was the shock and realization of everything this one accident caused.

If something was broken, how would I pay for the hospital bill? What about saving to go to St. John. What about my job? Could I still serve? It was summer, which was the best time of year at Pegasus. What was I going to do about rent? The pain would shoot throughout my body intermittently. Even though my wrists suffered the worst of it, my body, head included, was hit by the bike also when I went down.

Ariana's place was closer, but I knew that she'd have to leave for work soon and I didn't want to have to move soon again. The community clinic, where I knew I had to go, was closer to Bill's, where I was on my way to, so I decided to walk there. It took me a good half an hour to get there. When there weren't many cars going by, I'd allow myself to cry. I tried biking slowly a few times and discovered just how badly I was hurt. My wrists were shot.

At Bill's, I had the hardest time simply wiping myself in the bathroom. I cried myself to sleep, next to Bill, tears streaming down my face from all of the pain- physical, emotional and mental. I fell asleep instead of going straight to the clinic because I didn't want to go alone. No one in that house woke up before 11am, which was early for each of them. It was about 8:30am. The physical pain was manageable, as long as I didn't move my wrists at all.

Prior to my accident, I biked all over the city, doing yoga, swimming and workouts at a nearby gym that I biked to as well. Sometimes I worked out between doubles at work because it was fun and relaxing (the gym had a sauna and steam room in the pool area). I cried upon realization of every single thing that I could no longer do, like swimming, sauna or steam, which were at the top of my list of favorite things to do. The fact that I had to wear that cast for 5 weeks was the worst. I attempted to take it off a few times. I got so sick of having it on ALL the time. I don't keep ANY thing on my body that compares for I don't even wear jewelry most of the time. It drove me crazy.

At least I already had my plane ticket to move to St. John in 6 weeks or rather the money set aside for it. I moved into Bill and Derek's house, where Dick was staying for the summer. It was Dick telling us all about St. John that made me decide to go. My friends were all very helpful right after the accident. My wrists were too weak for me to comb my own hair, since it's so curly and oftentimes, takes a bit of effort. Derek combed it one day and Bill did it another. I could manage it myself after a few days, but at first I didn't have the strength. I could hardly believe it. It took a LONG time before I could do one push up comfortably, whereas before, I could do twenty "guy style" push-ups. I've healed almost 100% since.

I found someone to sublet my room on Alki for a month (our lease was up when I planned to leave). Fortunately, I found someone just in time and Mike, the one who recorded my music, hooked me up with a position in the Seattle Fringe Festival '03. It wasn't much money, but it was something I could do to make some money with a broken arm before moving. I worked 9 hours a day for 17 days straight, ending a day or 2 before I left with Dick and Bill from Seattle for St. John, USVI.

Before we get to that part though, let me once again, digress….

I hadn't been sexually involved with any one in any way since Nathan. During the six days between my unemployment denial and Pegasus, I contemplated being an escort for the first and only time in my life. A man wanted to bring me into his "entourage" to service his "upscale" clientele of doctor/lawyer types in five star hotels. I was to have my own driver and could make $10,000 in a weekend with some of these men. As poor as I was, and for as many women in the world who have done it, I was willing to at least seriously consider it for the money alone. I was broke as a joke and there was nothing funny about it.

I called Bill, told him what I was thinking and asked him if I could use him for practice. I've said many strange things to Bill. This is one that took the cake, even, and especially, for me. He was way freer with his body than I'd ever been, so he was rather surprised. He agreed to be my guinea pig. He told me that he didn't think it was a good idea for me to be an escort, but he'd still have sex with me.

Bill is a relatively attractive guy who is one of my best friends that I trust and adore. I had too difficult a time even thinking about us touching sexually without my desire. The idea of an unattractive, stinky man giving me any amount of money to touch me in any way when I didn't feel like it was awful. I was repulsed and that was the end of that. Sometimes I have to at least seriously explore an idea in my mind before putting it to rest, even if I know that the chances are slim that it'll go anywhere. Some of my best creations have come about that way. It all begins in the imagination.

Over the years, Bill has watched my personality and body go through some major transformations. This was no exception. In the spring of '03 I was so active and happy. Summer was coming and my energy was alluring. It had been a while since he had sex so sometimes he asked me half jokingly if I would have sex with him. I considered having sex with Bill for his birthday – in mid March, but I just wasn't feeling it. Around that time I thought, "I'd be perfectly content to never have sex again."

Ariana and I started getting together every week, back in January or so, for her to read "The Lord of the Rings" trilogy to me. Her brother read it to her when she was young and she read it to her sisters. She adored the trilogy. I saw the first two movies and loved them which made me excited to hear it. I had known her family for close to ten years at that point. They were a tight knit group. Reading this book with Ariana made me feel closer to all of them.

Many things in life aren't simply about "the act", it's everything that "that act" encompasses. Ariana would bring food, usually bread and cheese, for that's what the hobbits ate. I usually provided drink. She rarely drank alcohol, but those hobbits did! We'd run off together into another world almost every week for 9 months. I'm so glad that I did, for Goldberry and Tom Bombadil are two of my favorite characters that were never mentioned in the movies, along with a host of others, whom I never would have known of otherwise. I'm grateful for the movie version as well as the books. Having them read to me throughout that year created many memorable and sacred experiences.

Being read to took some getting used to for no one had ever read to me before, not that I remember anyway. Juliet was the only person with whom I read a whole book aloud. We read "The Little Prince" to each other the first year that we lived together. That book is a part of my soul forever, for numerous reasons. It makes me smile just thinking about it. "'What is essential is invisible to the eye.', the little Prince repeated, so that he was sure to remember."

Juliet knew that Ariana and I were getting together every week to read. She and Ariana were still close. I think that Ariana reading to me made Juliet a little jealous. Juliet had been seeing a therapist for a couple of years and decided to contact me sometime in the spring because she was finally ready to talk to me directly and honestly. I accepted her invitation to sit in a park one day and talk. We're not best friends again, but at least we are friends. We can hug sincerely and catch up in each other's lives in open and loving ways.

Sometime in April, Bill stayed over my place and woke up aroused. It was a gorgeous morning. For whatever reason, I happened to be turned on too. We slept in the same bed countless times, half the time naked, without anything happening. This time was different and so it began-our 6 month sexual involvement. We didn't have sex right away, shortly thereafter though. It had been a year and a half since I kissed anyone or had sex. More than anything, I thought that Bill would be easy to deal with sexually because we knew each other so well. We loved and trusted each other already.

That was the third period of our lives, and longest, that we were sexually involved. It was also, by far, the best sex we ever had with each other. I doubt I would've waited so long if I had known how much better a lover he had become. I think his attitude had a lot to do with it. He was more positive and nurturing to himself and as a friend during that time. Sweetness is an aphrodisiac for me. Bill and I weren't romantically involved at any point. He's the closest I've ever come to a "fuck buddy". I don't use that term with him though because he is so much more than that to me.

He was one of my best friends of 9 years, my "BOYEE", someone whom I relaxed and chilled with and trusted to be honest with me, even if he looked like an asshole. I think that it was the combination of all of these things that made him the first person I had sex with that brought me to orgasm by vaginal intercourse alone. I was VERY pleasantly surprised!! Neither of us intended it. Perhaps it was all of that time without sex too. "If you give a starving person a cracker, it'll be the best cracker in the world!" (Eddie Murphy- "Raw") Our sex was awesome and we had little bullshit to weed through, at first.

The last person that Bill had sex with before me was Alannah, Ariana's sister, the previous summer. I think Alannah was in Japan at the time for work. She was due to return to Seattle in August. She and Bill still had strong feelings for each other from their brief time together, but they made no promises of monogamy while they were apart. I told Alannah (she and I kept in touch via email) that I had sex with Bill. She didn't seem bothered by it. Bill and I entertained the idea of all of us together, but didn't think that would go over well in actuality. We knew we had to stop having sex before Alannah got back.

The first time I was ready to stop having sex with Bill was when he realized that he forgot to tell me that he had sex with another friend of his (whom he recently met) without a condom. He told me that they had sex the day after it happened. I forgot to ask about protection. I assumed he used protection because we didn't, since I was on Depo Provera (birth control) and we were having sex regularly and exclusively up until that point. That's when I first attempted to pull away from Bill sexually, for that was some asinine shit.

I was shocked to discover that he was that careless with our lives (diseases) and emotions for he hadn't mentioned me to her at all. She was falling in love with him and I wasn't in love with him like that and it caused a bunch of drama to ensue between him and her and our circle of friends that could've been prevented. That didn't stop us though.

Not even the time that he came home (this was after I'd broken my arm) and told me that he almost had sex with one of the women he was waiting on in the bathroom at the restaurant where he worked. The most disturbing part of that story was that he said it was the fact that he had tables to tend to that prevented him from having sex with her, NOT the fact that he didn't have a condom. PERHAPS that was simply the FIRST reason he thought of- I gave him the benefit of the doubt on that one (barely). It had to end.

It dawned on me that the man, my friend, whom I thought had become discriminating with his lovers because he learned to love himself more had simply not been getting enough attention. Summer was upon us. Clothing was being shed. Bill had a weakness for women's flirtations, as many men do. I didn't begrudge him his fun. I asked that he be careful along the way. I did my best to stop having sex with him because I didn't trust him to be as discriminating as I wanted a lover to be, plus Alannah was returning shortly. It wasn't a good idea for us to have sex with each other anymore, but it was so easy and felt so good that it was difficult to stop. The fact that Alannah was coming back in 2 weeks is what finally did get us to stop, briefly.

Dick was in Seattle visiting from St. John for the summer to have a break from his ex-girlfriend and the island. He stayed with Derek and Bill and was there when I moved in after my accident. It was a very crowded house and some crazy times went on there. I was on survival mode, especially once I began working 17 days in a row. I was dealing with Bill's craziness (in general, but in particular, over Alannah's return), our sexual relationship, my lack of money, moving to an island (I looked forward to it, but knew no one and trusted Dick very little) and my friends, who were mainly in the food and/or entertainment industry generally went to sleep as the sun came up.

Few were compassionate about the HUGE lifestyle change that I underwent in such a short amount of time. I felt very isolated at times and craved a sanctuary of my own, but had none, not even my journal, for it hurt to write for more than a few minutes at a time. We were performing a bunch of shows before we left too, since it was summer and Bill was about to leave. He played the bass with 4 or 5 people on their various songs. Everyone was in their own world. I wish I at least had a room to call my own- one that allowed me time to be quiet.

I went from sharing a bed with Bill to sharing one with Derek (platonically), once Alannah came home. It was a weird adjustment, but mainly because I was so miserable over everything that had happened in such a short period of time. I also knew that our friends because of Alannah's return were watching me for they knew that Bill and I were having sex. Tonjia and Amber were two of my only friends who knew that I wanted nothing more with Bill and that I had no problem with Alannah and he being together. They were a big part of my life support then. Derek knew too, but was in his own shit, as was Ariana who wasn't sure what to believe because she was so out of it due to several reasons and so close to the situation with Alannah being her sister and Bill a close friend. She was also sad that Bill and I were moving so far away.

It was one of the most depressing times of my life. I wasn't about to slit my wrists, they'd been through enough! I just wanted some calm and tranquility of some sort. Between my work schedule and the chaos of that house, peace felt non-existent in my life. I was sleep deprived (which can make me very cranky), malnourished (I ate very cheaply), dehydrated (I'm sure), smoking cigarettes and drinking alcohol- all things that make me an unhappy person anyway, but especially when experienced daily.

Some of my closest friends like Ariana and Bill didn't understand what was wrong with me since they handle life much differently. It had been a while since I lived in that kind of environment. As much as I wanted to enjoy my time there, I counted down the days until we left so I could rest in peace- literally!

My last couple of days, I got my cast cut off (HAPPILY!!! I had dreams of ripping it off) and spent what time I could with close friends, for I didn't know when I would be in Seattle again. Things were awkward between Bill and Alannah because of me, which annoyed me.

They worried so much about my reaction after I told them that I don't care if they have sex. I was in a pissy mood for many other reasons that had nothing to do with their sex life. I didn't want any of it (my miserable life or their sex) to be an issue, but it was. Bill was about to leave with me and Dick to go live on a tropical island, for at least 6 months, which might sound good, but it didn't make sense.

I suggested to Bill that he follow his heart and do what he felt was best. I knew how much he cared for Alannah and didn't want him to feel like he would be letting me down as a roommate, friend or lover if he chose to stay in Seattle. Dick reacted more like the jealous and hurt lover. He wanted his good friend on the island with him, which was understandable, but selfish. That is characteristic of Dick. He was also known to cheat friends out of money. I'd loaned him $650 shortly before I broke my arm because I believed he was a changed man. He was supposed to pay me back once we got back to the island. I was a little nervous about that after I broke my arm.

Even though I knew I wouldn't live in Seattle again for a long time, if ever, I was excited to move away from my surroundings and make a new life for myself on the island of St. John. My plan was to live and work there for 9 months and save up enough money to do a week long film workshop in Florence, Italy the following June. Dick told me that the money made as a server on the island was enough to be able to do this.

I had been planning to go some place warm for the winter that year anyway. I had Brazil in mind, not to make money, just to live cheaply. My friend Tom married a Brazilian woman within a year of things ending with Tiffany. Tom lived in Brazil for three months and absolutely loved it! His wife's family would gladly host me whenever I chose to visit. St. John was a better alternative at that time, since it's a U.S. territory with lots of tourism where I could be warm during the winter while working.

Dick, Bill and I are all from Philadelphia, so we flew back for one week to see friends and family before flying to St. John-well, St. Thomas really. There are no airports on St. John, only ferries go there. One day, while at Dick's parent's house, Bill and I had a long conversation about how we weren't going to have sex anymore since we hadn't for a good 3 weeks or so, only to conclude by having sex- in Dick's parents house- before we left. It was like an addiction, "I'm gonna kick tomorrow…" (Jane's Addiction "Jane Says").

Chapter 4
Welcome to Love City

When we first arrived on the island of St. Thomas, three things surprised me: the steep hills, the greenery of the landscape and how many black people were there. I don't know why, but I'd imagined mainly white people living there. I suppose it's because that's what I'd seen in most photos of the Caribbean that showcased the beaches and tourist activities. I never paid close attention or really thought about it. It was a welcome surprise because I'd never lived among another culture of black people before. I became fascinated and fell in love with Caribbean culture.

I had no idea what I was to encounter upon arrival. Dick was returning to the island after his first year living there with his girlfriend, who was from Philly too, but I didn't meet her until I arrived on island. They were no longer together. Dick's parents are the ones who exposed them to the island when they all vacationed together. Within two years, they moved there.

All three of us were staying in Dick's ex-girlfriend's studio. Bill and I continued to have sex. We were all looking for work and a place to live. Dick had no money and owed me $650. Bill had the most, at around $1000. I think I had around $500. Food is expensive on the island. Most things in the supermarkets are imported, so they cost more than what we were used to paying. Cigarettes and alcohol are much cheaper, but we did our best not to "vacation" too much for all of us needed to make money as soon as possible. Bill was doing his best not to drink every day, but our situation, all around, was not helping him in his decision to drink less alcohol.

Between mid-August and mid-October (height of hurricane season), many restaurants and shops shut down. We got there mid-September to have a better chance at finding a place to live. The island was pretty quiet. The new batch of people had yet to arrive. We were the very first to trickle in that year. Someone Dick knew had just bought a restaurant and had asked him and Bill to help get it together while they looked for work and housing.

Dick's ex recommended me to a woman that she had worked for almost her entire year there. So I started working, almost immediately, in a fancy gift shop with all kinds of beautiful things set up in a relatively small area. I was paid cash once a week, listened to my own music and worked by myself most times, so I was content with that job for a few months.

Within the first week, Bill's misery had grown to the point where he decided to go back to Seattle. I was not at all surprised. I'd always supported the idea, much to Dick's dismay. It grew evident that Bill had left his heart behind, not just in leaving Alannah, but also in leaving all of his friends (he was a central figure in his group of friends), his neighborhood (he had his "routine places"), and his bands (he was a bassist to many). He thought that being in St. John would allow him to save money and practice the bass in a beautiful environment, but Bill didn't realize just how much he had until they were gone. One of the lines from a favorite book that I often quote to Bill is from Khalil Gibran's, "The Prophet" fits well with this situation- "Sometimes the mountain is clearer to the climber from the plain." So true.

I walked Bill to the ferry dock the morning of his departure. It marked the ending of an era between us. Never had we been as close as we were that year. It was quite a journey. I loved him dearly, but welcomed the space between us, for his energy is an intense one, with many darker shades and corners to explore than my own, that I did not care to explore, at least not as his lover- a reason why I saw some of these darker sides in ways I never had before. At times, Bill and I could be a lot for each other to handle, but we loved one another like family and wished each other well with some sadness, but no tears.

Once back in Seattle and settled, Bill was a bit unsure about bringing Alannah up with me, which hurt my feelings a bit because I thought he knew me better, but once he did, he saw that I clearly had no issue, and as usual, it was easy for us to talk about anything, like some of the boys that I met. Our communication was steady and open while I was in St. John, which pleased me for I did not want our sexual involvement to ruin our friendship in any way and I felt it had come really close, too close.

After Bill left, Dick and I moved in with his friend who was opening the restaurant along with his wife and daughter. We stayed with them for a few weeks during which time I was hired at a "casual, fine dining, Italian" restaurant called "Café Roma" in downtown Cruz Bay, which was only about 8 blocks long. I waited tables 3-5 nights of the week and worked at the gift shop once or twice a week.

One of the dishwashers at Café Roma told me about an apartment that was close by, within walking distance, and pretty cheap, by St. John standards. Housing is HARD to find and EXPENSIVE. It's like a tropical Manhattan. It was a small one bedroom for $650/mo with no hot water. We took it. Dick had his bed in the living room. I had mine (a single) in the tiny bedroom where the walls didn't even go all the way up to the ceiling. Dick would come home at 3am or 4am, at times, and blast his music like he didn't have good sense (an aspiring dj).

The men out number the women on St. John something ridiculous, like 7 to 1. I was happy to be single again and was not looking to be anybody's girlfriend or to have anyone be my boyfriend or lover. There was one guy that I was attracted to that came into the restaurant regularly. I always wondered why I was attracted to him. There wasn't much about him, but there was something. We had interesting conversations at times and I knew he liked me more than he let on.

I met a guy named Luke one night at a favorite local bar. He would not say some word that his friend wanted him to say. It wasn't that bad either. Luke's friend asked me if I could get him to say it ("buttfuck"). He wouldn't. It was his friend's last night on island and this was how Luke and I were introduced. I was surprised that Luke just wouldn't say the word, but he was determined not to for no good reason other than the fact that he didn't want to which I respected. I thought he was funny and a nice guy, but he didn't stick out to me in any way afterwards.

Come to find out, he filled in as a cook at Café Roma from time to time because he used to cook there for 5 years. I had fun working with him on the nights that he worked. He was really nice and got along well with almost everyone (except for the one guy that almost no one liked). Café Roma was a small place. We rotated between 4 servers most nights. They weren't open for lunch. It was a local favorite. They had the best pizza on the island as well as the most generous portions of some of the tastiest Italian food you'll find on the island, at reasonable prices too, inexpensive by most island restaurant standards.

One day, Luke offered to take me sailing. It was sometime in December '03. I'd never been sailing before. There were boats all around St. John. Some people, like Luke, lived on their boat ("boaties"). After our first day sailing, I was hooked. The bartender at Roma owned a boat and lived on it too. He said that I was going to fall in love with Luke- something about sailors and the first time they take a woman sailing. He wanted to be my first, even though he had a girlfriend. I didn't believe him, about falling in love with a sailor. Luke seemed like a nice and cool guy, but I was certainly not falling in love- or so I thought.

I was so in love with sailing after my first time. It's an incredible feeling to feel the wind carry you and to manipulate it to do what you aim to do with your vessel. It's incredibly soothing and quiet, for Luke's motor was broken, so there were never any foreign sounds other than the stereo. Being out on the water, surrounded by so much beauty and traveling at the same time was an experience like no other. I could happily sail every day.

Luke owned a 1945 wooden sailboat (28'), which is rare to see in the Caribbean. It's a John Alden (name of the architect/designer), which is usually found in the New England area. He put many hours of hard work and care into that boat. Shortly after our first (maybe second) sail together, he invited me to join him on a trip to Virgin Gorda, a British Virgin Island about 6-8 hours away by boat.

He asked me if I wanted to stay the night there for a couple of days during our Christmas break since the restaurant was closed and neither of us had plans. I was a little apprehensive to spend that much time on his narrow boat after only knowing him a short while, however, he seemed so nice that I felt he'd be okay with me doing whatever I wanted, which is all I wanted to do- to enjoy my free time doing whatever I felt like doing. It was the first time I had any real time off since I first arrived, which I could enjoy only so much due to lack of funds.

We had a fantastic time in Virgin Gorda. Luke brought some chocolate mushrooms that we took on Christmas and hung out on gigantic rocks, jumping in and out of the clearest blue waters, all day. It was the first REAL vacation I'd had in too long of a time. Luke was a perfect gentleman. I'd told him before we left that I don't date and that I wasn't looking for anything romantic. He didn't seem phased. We genuinely had a good time together and I wasn't concerned about his intentions. It baffled me that we were around each other so much, at times drinking, and in such close quarters with me in a bikini, yet sex was never an issue. This is when I realized that I was developing feelings for this man. He was so nice, respectful and considerate of me as a friend. He also did some really sweet things too, but without expectations, at least not immediate ones.

Once back to shore, I came home and nursed what was the start of my second (thankfully, last) boil- on my right butt cheek! Boils HUUUUUURT!!! They hurt progressively for days (never had one before or after St. John). Luke invited me to join him on his boat for New Year's, but I opted to stay at home, due to my boil that was about to burst any minute, and to do what I've done on New Year's Eve for so many years in the past- orgasmically bring in the New Year by my own hands. Afterwards, I watched the fireworks from outside my door. Dick was out somewhere for most of the night.

The next time Luke and I went out for a sail, we sailed from Johnson's Bay to Salt Pond (another shore on St. John), which only took about two hours. There were only one or two other boats around, in a very large and beautiful area. It was all so amazing- the different fish, sea turtles, starfish and such. On the way back to Johnson's bay, shortly before we were to tie to the mooring, Luke kissed me. I told him the day before that he could. Why he waited that long, I do not know. It took us a bit to relax into one another, but eventually we did. We could kiss for hours. I never grew tired of it. Kissing Luke never got "old".

Luke and I took some getting used to each other. I did my best to explain to him my philosophy behind not wanting to use the term "boyfriend". I kissed two other guys within a month though, which was a bit unsettling to him. It was the timing. I wouldn't have kissed them if I had his trust. His distrust of me is why I wasn't "with him" during those times. Both incidences occurred within a 4-6 week span.

The thing is, Luke was the only person I really wanted to be with romantically. It was because we weren't together, when I kissed the other guys, that I even considered kissing the other guys. They were cute, smart and interesting, but Luke and I had magic together. To me it seemed obvious that I would rather be with him, and only him. I wanted him to trust me beyond the label of "boyfriend/girlfriend", to know that I was with him every single day because I wanted to be, not because I had to be and that I greatly valued his trust. I had no intentions of exploiting or abusing it.

We weren't "together" when he got with one of his sister's friends who was visiting during a time we chose to be "just friends". The only thing that upset me in regards to her was that he willingly performed oral sex on her when I had such an issue with him and oral sex. I regularly shaved, upon his request, and still, pretty much nothing! It had been over 7 years since I had any sort of outbreak and I'm very clean. Come on! I wasn't asking for one orgasm, let alone the multiple that I'm capable of, I was just asking for some attention! I had every right to as well, for almost every morning I happily woke him up with fellatio, sometimes leading to more. It took me a minute to get over him and his sister's friend, for that was not cool by me. However, love is about forgiveness as well and I knew by then that I was totally in love with Luke. I would work something out with him as best I could to appease both of us.

Finally, around June, our relationship reached this level where our trust for one another was solidified and we became a cohesive unit without the title. We made each other extremely happy and it took very little effort, for we both put a lot of effort into our individual lives, which made sharing our lives together easier for us to enjoy. There were areas that could use some work, but we constantly looked forward to spending time together and the time that we did spend together seemed to go by too quickly all the time. We had numerous trips planned in our heads.

In April, my good friend Laura, whom I worked with at Café Roma, decided to move back to Vermont and asked me if I wanted to move into her apartment. It was three times the size and three times nicer than my place with Dick. It was $100 more, but I could afford it (barely). Mom and my oldest nephew, Erik planned on visiting in May and they would've been cramped with me and Dick. It was perfect! She planned to leave it furnished for me. It had two sets of hurricane proof doors that led to the balcony overlooking Cruz Bay. A couch fit comfortably on the balcony, which is where I spent many afternoons staring out at the inspiring skies and waters of the Caribbean.

I left the restaurant around the end of March. I got tired of serving. At the same time, I began picking up hours at a nearby gym. It didn't pay a lot, but it was very easy, I got to shower and wash clothes for free (VERY BIG deal on an island where water is a precious commodity) and workout for free. Laura gave me her apartment, cell phone and her job. She was selling sarongs from the pool hut on the Westin's property for a woman who flew to Indonesia throughout the year to purchase materials. The owner was a best friend to the owner of Café Roma.

My third job (I had to get a third one to make sure I made $750/mo) was as an administrative assistant for a place that rented vacation home rentals. I helped confirm the car rentals, airport meet ups and suggested places to eat, etc. alongside general office duties. The office was located on the slow side of the island, Coral Bay, close to where Luke kept his boat. It was much quieter in Coral Bay. There were dramatic views and hiking trails all over. Goats, chickens, horses, iguanas, cows and pigs would roam around like it was nothing.

Hitchhiking is very common on the island. Just stick your finger out and point which ever direction you care to go when a car goes by and at some point, someone will stop and give you a ride. There was a bus that ran once an hour, but not always. It ran up and down the main road (there are only 3 roads on the whole island) until 8pm or so (I know! Crazy, right?). Luke got a jeep sometime in late July. Before, we hitched, took the bus or got rides. Once, I left my shoes on Luke's boat and didn't realize it until he had pulled off in the dinghy- the small, inflated boat used to go from the boat to the dock or shore. I went all day without having to wear any shoes, while working at two places and taking the bus. It was the funniest thing! I love St. John for that. I took life there very seriously, but only so seriously because of things like that.

One of my best friends named Jade, whom I'd met over the phone in Seattle while I was living with Dean in 2000, came to visit me in January '04. We got off to a rocky start because I was stressed out and she brought a guy with her at the last minute, which upset me. So often when we made plans in the past with just the two of us, some guy ended up coming along whom she didn't even care that much about, if she cared about him at all, which is why I was not happy to hear of her last minute Puerto Rican addition. This guy turned out to be really cool though. They ended up kissing for the first time on the plane going to Puerto Rico and ended up staying together for a few years. Her vacation ended on a very good note. It was awesome having her there.

Mom and Erik are the only family members who visited me on St. John. I was glad that Erik, at 16, got a chance to see the way another culture, especially another black culture, can live. He and mom were tripped out by all of the hills. They were nervous about driving around the cliffs. They made me a little nervous at first too, but I quickly got used to them. Neither of them wanted to go the beach much, if at all. They were more into the oddities of the island. My nephew was mainly interested in the girls, styles and basketball.

I took mom to see the boutique I used to work in, for she loved those kinds of things, and I left with one of the cutest bundles of joy ever to come into my life. His name is Bob- short for Bobcat. He was only 7 weeks old. The owner had him in a box in the store. He was an island stray. He had the most adorable body (part brown-point Siamese) and bluest eyes with a meow that made me want to keep him with me always. I couldn't have pets in my apartment, so I ended up giving him to my good friend Mani, but not for a good month or so. I took him to work with me, to the beach, on the ferry (with mom and Erik to say goodbye) and all over that island. He's traveled more than many I know! He now lives in Atlanta with Mani's mom.

Every year, around the first week of June through the first week of July, is St. John's Carnival. It's a month long celebration that culminates right around July 4th, which marks the day that the slaves who lived there were emancipated. This woman Rebecca asked me what I thought of her idea to sell tee shirts at Carnival. We decided in early May that we were going to sell tee shirts and crafts at a table during Carnival for 2 weeks out of the 4. She drew the designs for the tee shirts. They ended up being a big attraction for us.

We got everything together, made our crafts, secured the spot (we paid $10/day) and sold our items on a daily basis up to the day before the last day. The last day we would've had to pay $50 to rent space and we were beat by then since we were both working at our normal jobs while having our table. We didn't make a lot of money, but I'm glad that we did it. It was a valuable learning and growing experience for us both on many levels. One of the best things we both got from it was a strong sense of community and bonding with other vendors who came and set up shop every day alongside us.

Shortly after carnival ended, Luke abruptly left on a boat trip with a couple of friends to deliver a yacht to Grenada- an island at the bottom of a chain of islands ending right above South America. He thought he'd be gone a week. It ended up being 3 weeks. It was the first time we'd been apart for that long. I missed him terribly and could hardly wait for his phone calls, for he had no phone at sea. I had to wait until he arrived on land. The constant uncertainty was the hardest to handle. Not knowing when I'd hear from him or how long he'd be gone the entire duration of those 3 weeks was painstaking!

While Luke was gone, my brother and I were emailing back and forth and talking when we could. He was going through some extremely challenging life changes, professionally as well as personally. Also, Erik failed algebra, which caused him to have to repeat a grade. I knew that there was only so much I could do from St. John. I had faith that my brother would work things out eventually, but more than anything, I felt a strong pull to be more active in the lives of my nephews and my niece, as well as the rest of my family. I knew that only I could be as closely involved in all of their lives in the ways that I am, for I am family and there is no other me- period. It was time to go back to Philadelphia to live, at least temporarily.

It'd been about 8 years since I'd lived in Philly for any length of time, last time being when I stayed for a couple of months before returning to Seattle for the fifth time. I saw myself staying for the kids' school year. I planned to return to St. John to go down island (sail to Grenada and back) with Luke the following summer. We had talked about doing that trip before the summer came around that year, but we didn't save the money to make it happen. I wanted us to stay together while I was in Philly, visiting as often as possible, but I wasn't sure he'd go for that idea. I was really nervous about telling him.

I first told Luke that I was thinking about leaving while he was still at sea, which was not the best idea. Looking back, I wish that I waited to tell him. I wasn't used to keeping anything from him and it was weighing heavily on my mind and heart. Not knowing when he was coming back to St. John was TORTUOUS!! I was very sad at the reality of the situation and I was very anxious about Luke's reaction. I wasn't sure if he was going to break up with me because of my decision. We had a love that is rare and finally established trust between us. I wasn't going to turn my back on that, but would he?

When Luke returned, we were very happy to see each other, but I was set to leave in five weeks, September 7th. I'd booked my ticket and everything. I already told my landlady and employers. By the time Luke got back, I'd accepted my fate and was relieved to hear that he wanted to stay together. He didn't like the idea of being in a long distance relationship because his last one didn't work out. I figured that the time would go by fast due to us working, seeing each other every 2-3 months and it only being a total of 9 months that I'd be gone.

Slowly, as my departure date neared, Luke became more distant and not as sweet as I'd grown accustomed to him being. All the signs were there, but I didn't see it coming. Luke broke up with me one week before I left the island. It happened the morning of my first day of freedom- no work or anything planned in my life (other than my flight) indefinitely. I was eagerly waiting for that time to come since I had decided to leave, so that I could devote as much time as I could to friends, island exploration and Luke. I hadn't done much hanging out around the island pretty much since I'd arrived (workaholic tendencies). Many people came to St. John to vacation, now I was finally on vacation!

The first morning of my vacation, Luke broke my heart into a million pieces- not just by breaking up with me, but by the way he went about it. He wasn't nice to me. He wasn't compassionate. He was hurt and mad at me for deciding to leave (I didn't know or realize this part until later) and it came out as him being a cold asshole. I was confused and felt severely betrayed. I knew that he was resistant to the long distance relationship idea, but I didn't understand why he wasn't at least willing to give it a shot.

I tasted a strong bitter sweetness that lasted all day every day for my remaining days there. Everyone in my life knew how much I loved living on that island, as well as how much I loved my family and their importance in my life. Eye doctors and dentists aren't very good or cheap on the island, which was another reason to be in Philly for a bit. I was also going to look into becoming certified as a yoga teacher. My friends were all very supportive of my decision to return to Philly. Some respected and admired my decision. It was too much for Luke. I don't think he truly believed I'd return to St. John to live.

There was a hurricane warning my last days on the island. The sky was dark. People were securing things at businesses and at home, doing last minute shopping. I think Hurricane Ivan was threatening to hit. None of it mattered to me. Hurricane Luke had created havoc in my soul. I cried profusely that week. I hadn't had such sadness pour from me in so long. He just decided- boom, that's it, we're not together anymore and the worst was that he knew for weeks before he told me. The morning we broke up, I asked him to drop me off at a mutual friends' place. I knew they'd let me stay with them (two brothers) until I left. I had few places to go for I planned on staying with Luke on his boat the whole week.

On the day I left, Luke happened to be coming down the road into town at the exact time I was hitching a ride into town. He stopped to pick me up. I almost didn't get in, but no other cars were coming and another hitchhiker was in the car. We didn't talk most of the ride. When I was getting out, he asked to meet up later. We did and it was very emotional, heart wrenching and eye opening. As upset as I was with him for not being honest with me sooner, I was glad that he was at least finally being honest with me then. It was crazy, for a lot was happening so suddenly. Since Luke lived on his sailboat and the hurricane was close, he had the stress of that on his mind alongside all of this. It was an awful and very difficult time for both of us.

The night before I left, I met a man named Henry in Coral Bay. He asked to take me out to dinner before I got on my ferry to St. Thomas. I had no big plans and he let me pick the place I wanted to go. I chose a place I'd always wanted to dine in named Zo-Zo's. It had a terrific view of the sunset, with the restaurant situated atop the water. Luke and I stayed the night at the adjacent hotel just a couple of weeks prior. That's when I began to notice a serious change in his behavior. We had a terrible time when we could have had the time of our lives in a BEAUTIFUL vacation home. We either weren't talking or arguing (which was not common) almost the whole time. I'm not sure over what or how the arguing even began.

While at Zo-Zo's, and throughout my entire last week on the island, I did my very best to enjoy all of it for what it was worth. I wasn't used to feeling so upset all the time. I'd grown quite accustomed to feeling happy and in love during my time on the island. The sudden change came as a great shock to my system. Most people couldn't tell- unless they knew me. My light inside had dimmed dramatically to a small flame, not just because of Luke, but because I was leaving the best place I'd ever lived up to that point. At least I knew that island life was for me and I could return whenever I felt like it.

St. John had a population of about 3,500 residents. Approximately 1.5 million tourists visit every year. I was very happy that I experienced life there as a resident and not a tourist. By January it became evident to me that I wasn't going to have enough money saved to go to Italy for the film workshop that I wanted to do. Luke and I began talking about plans for the summer sometime in February. Many sailors who own boats sail their boats down island to avoid hurricanes because they're less likely to be hit by a hurricane at one of the islands further south on the chain, like Grenada (which actually did get hit that year). I still hoped we could possibly do the trip the next summer.

Island life was the closest I came to "small town" life. I began to know and recognize names and faces, as they did mine. Many locals say, "Good Morning/Afternoon/Evening", which I love. I befriended several Rastafarians with open, caring hearts- those who were true to Rastafarian ways of living. I saw a couple that I got to know become pregnant and bear a child, a boy. I felt so honored to have touched my friend Toneya's stomach while her baby was in her womb. She was born and raised on St. John, as was her husband, which, oddly enough, are rare to meet. Many St. Johnians don't interact with people who aren't West Indian unless they have to, especially the women.

West Indian women aren't seen out often at night on St. John, especially past a certain age. It's commonly known and accepted that West Indian men "mess around" with more than one woman at a time, but it's usually kept secret (as in other cultures). I've also heard that

West Indian women tend to have a thing against tourist women because the tourist women are so easily lured by the West Indian men that it makes keeping their men monogamous very difficult.

With all of that said, I was generally embraced by the West Indian women on St. John. I look forward to seeing three in particular, upon my return. One is my first landlady, Miss Ina. I gave her a couple of full body massages because she was overworked and stressed. She's a very nice woman, possibly in her sixties. I was surprised she let me massage her! She was totally relaxed with me in her home- and I'd only known her about 2 or 3 months. I was very happy to have her trust. We got along fabulously, even after I moved out. She understood my reasons for leaving. I asked Dick to move out a few times, but there was nothing he could afford and no good roommate situations. Thus, when Laura's place opened up, it seemed like a dream! Toneya is another of the 3 West Indian women I'd love to see again.

The third is a Diva- for real! It's used in a good sense though. Her voice soars through her effortlessly. I met Lacreesha while working in the pool hut at the Westin. We both worked in there. I sold sarongs while she gave out towels to the guests. We got to know each other and had a lot of fun at work. I saw her perform at a couple of places on St. John as well as St. Thomas. Her band's (Ah We Band) music always made me want to dance and enjoy myself. I still listen to them now and look forward to seeing them again. She was only 21 years old, with a 3-year-old daughter, yet her spirit was full of life and energy, while working at the Westin and many long hours of singing. She's an inspiration to me.

There were many people that I got along with easily. My closest friends were those I met at Café Roma. I became really close with a couple of people from there- Laura, Luke, the boys I stayed with my last week there, Sappho (a female dishwasher from Dominica) and Tracy. Tracy and I started hiking St. John's many trails that are part of National Park territory, towards the end of my stay. We'd hike, picnic, hike some more, then end up at a beach, where we swam and rested until we went home. It was magnificent!

The National Park's land is why housing's so expensive. St. John is incredibly beautiful because in 1956, Laurence Rockefeller purchased 5,000 acres (three quarters of the island) and preserved it as National Park property. In some ways this is a terrific thing, in some ways, it is terrible. It's good for people like you and me, who go to visit and explore, for we are ignorant of its history. Many locals lost parts, if not all of their land due to this division and allotment of property. Imagine if your land was suddenly "National Park Property" without being given a dime. Now imagine if someone paid your neighbor $500,000 for a half-acre of land with only grass on it and you still had nothing because the government said so.

The fact that St. John was such an expensive place to buy property created an influx of wealthy people, mostly Americans, who visited the island. Many bought homes and rented them out to vacationers throughout the year. That's usually how they made their money back from the purchase of the property, especially with so few hotels on the island. The Westin's cheapest is around $250/nt. Caneel Bay's cheapest was around $600/nt. Campgrounds start around $90/nt and those are OFF-season prices! It was oftentimes more beneficial to go with a couple of friends and share a villa for a week. A villa is a home that's rented out on a weekly basis, similar to a hotel (longer stays), but nicer amenities and more privacy. Villas usually worked out to be less money.

Snorkeling was one of my favorite things to do on the island that I didn't do until Dick's parents, who visited in May, made me put on a mask and do it. It was SO MUCH FUN!!! I loved it! I look forward to doing it again! Luke had urged me to do it sooner, but I'd never been in the mood. I didn't think it'd be that great and in the winter, I didn't get in the water much. It was a little chilly for me to go in the water during the winter months. I have to be very hot to get wet and lie in the sun, especially if there are any breezes. I get cold very easily.

As I think I've made obvious, I didn't leave St. John because I was unhappy. I left St. John due to a tremendous sense of duty to my heart. I'm happiest overall when I work with it, not against it.

Chapter 5

Yo! City of Brotherly Love!

"The plan" was to live with my brother, help out with bills, help the kids in school (no failing grades!) and save some money. Then I was going to figure out where I wanted to go next and what I wanted to do from there. Upon first arrival, the weather was cloudy and rainy for weeks due to successive hurricanes. It was the year that Florida got hit 3 or 4 times back to back ('04). Philadelphia kept getting the residuals. When I left St. John, I wasn't sure I'd be able to fly out that day due to a hurricane warning. That same hurricane's residuals made it up to Philly about 3-4 weeks later, which made it gloomy for weeks with the city constantly overcast or rainy.

Luke and I were talking well enough, but he wasn't bending on us being together while apart. I didn't understand why it was so hard for him to be in a long distance relationship. He didn't have anyone else in mind that he wanted to be with anyway. We clearly still had strong feelings for each other. It felt like we were together, whether we wanted to be or not, but that, due to his decision, would not last for long. I was very sad about the whole thing.

Henry, the man that I met the night before I left St. John and who took me to Zo-Zo's, planned to move to New York a month after my departure. He was nervous about the move because he had lived on the island for 5 or 6 years and loved it very much. He was moving back to New York to legally divorce his wife and to be closer to his young children. It was a huge transition for him and he was clearly not looking forward to it, even though he could see the advantages that the move offered.

He was happy to have met me during that time. He was looking for something romantic with me for a little while, even though I made it abundantly clear that I wasn't interested in him that way (I'd learned to be completely up front with men from the get go). Once he made it to New York, we kept in touch here and there. I haven't talked to him in almost a year. During my first 30 days in Philly though, it was very nice and comforting to have Henry to talk to about all of the major changes going on around me, since he was the only person I knew who understood what it was like to live on the island and in a major city on the east coast and to have your heart broken.

Three weeks after I moved into my brother's place, I moved out of it and into my grandmother's 2-bedroom apartment. My brother made me so upset one day. He got angry with me for calling Erik's school to find out something that Erik asked me to find out. I had told the school that I was his legal guardian. My brother did not like that. His authority felt threatened. The title of guardian didn't matter to me, which I thought was obvious. I aimed to help out as best I could where I could. Erik had asked my brother to do the same thing I did and he procrastinated, so he asked me. Mind you, my brother didn't have a problem with me going to my youngest nephew's parent-teacher night when he couldn't make it. He can be really moody (cancer), but he's WAY better than he used to be!

I enjoy going on class trips, helping out with homework, going to awards ceremonies (okay, those can be really boring) and such. I wanted to be involved, however, I knew then that I could only be so involved in their lives in that regard. After I moved out and things settled down between my brother and I, we got along fine. I stayed with my grandmother for 2 and a half months. Let me tell you, those months were some of the hardest I'd experienced in my life in a very, very long time.

My grandmother means a whole lot to me. I love her with all of my heart. She can be really mean though and charismatic all in the same breath. She gets great joy out of being this way most of the time. She's creative, funny and sharp witted, especially for a financially poor, bed-ridden, 84 year old woman. She inspires me and can also infuriate me to no end. I give her all that I can, accept that it won't be enough and do my best to love her regardless of what she says or does.

Nana (what I call my grandmother) had an extra room with a bed in her apartment. I knew I wanted to work and live in the area where her apartment building was located, which was in the same projects where I grew up. They'd been renovated, so they're cleaner and nicer than before. She oftentimes can use another hand around her place, so I thought it'd be a good idea for us to live together. Her rent was very cheap, so I gave her what money I could when I could. My second landlady in St. John was being extremely difficult in giving me back my deposit. She ended up giving me $120 out of $750 (almost a month later) and wouldn't even mail the check! I asked Henry to pick it up for me and mail it to me, which he did.

Thankfully, my first landlady knew me well and gave me my half of the security deposit from when Dick and I lived together. He told me that he had to think about giving me my half. I was infuriated at his audacity. This was never discussed- him keeping my deposit- over the days/months it was known that he was moving out of that place. Unfortunately for me, I never changed the phone bill to his name and he stuck me with a $100 phone bill. That marked the beginning of the end for us.

According to horror stories I've heard from other friends about Dick, I made out very well!! He paid off the $650 he owed me over 9 months, which was terrific. To not even discuss keeping my deposit was not terrific. He's a myspace friend now, but that's it. He's in my group of friends, so he'll always be around. In fact, he's now living with Derek in Seattle. I keep people like him at a distance until they've shown me that they've changed and are trustworthy.

A few times, while we were living together, Dick would beg me to let him perform oral sex on me. He couldn't understand why I didn't want him to do that for me. He's a Leo. I think the idea that someone would refuse free head baffled him. He once said "You had sex with Bill, but you won't let me go down on you?" and I said, "I HAD sex with Bill- and wouldn't again at this point (due to all the bullshit we went through) and I trust Bill. I don't trust you."

If Dick was a cool, chill guy that I trusted and he wanted to give me head, I might have let him at that time in my life (I wasn't with Luke yet). Dick had run off at the mouth too many times though, to me and to too many others, so I only shared with him things that I didn't mind anyone, and possibly everyone, knowing. At this point, I'm comfortable enough with everything I've done in my past to talk about pretty much anything. Some things I'm more comfortable with than others. Just because I did something once doesn't mean I'd recommend it or do it again- even if I did it numerous times, like smoking commercial cigarettes or living with certain personality types (slobs, alcoholics, racists- no).

So I moved in with my grandmother in October '05. That month I began working at 4 or 5 places within a few weeks. Nana lives within easy walking or biking distance to many places in center city. I was hired as a hostess on a chic-chic, fine dining, 3 mast boat called the "Moshulu", docked at Penn's Landing. It seats 300 people. When I first walked in its beauty took me back. I fell in love immediately. In ways, I wish I'd never worked there, but in other ways, I'm so glad that I did, or else I never would've seen what I saw of the boat. I worked part-time for a little more than a month. The weather was usually cold, so I didn't check out the deck as much as I would've had it been warmer.

One of the coolest things about being involved with a sailor is that I learned how to sail and appreciate boats in ways I never thought I would. It always stands out to me that Joshua had a thing for boats and how odd that was to me. Having a boat had never occurred to me on my own, yet they now seemed to always be around me. They seem extravagant, but if you live on an island, like St. John, it's quite the opposite. Boaties are oftentimes seen by people living on land as being more like "hippies", "travelers", "adventurers" and for some, "trailer trash". Boaties are a version of "middle class" in the Caribbean. It's the cheapest way to own your home on St. John. It can be very stressful around hurricane season though and it's a lot of work taking care of a boat, therefore I never saw myself being a true boatie.

I loved that about Luke- that he had such passion for his boat, the water and sailing, enough to make all of the work involved worth it. Even on St. John, I hardly met any people who had that sense of exploration and adventure in them. Luke went sailing as often as he could. Since he didn't have a motor, it made coming in to shore and catching the mooring rather challenging at times. That never deterred him though. It explains how and why we worked so well together. We enjoy reaping the rewards of our hard labors. Both of us reveled in glee during our days off, usually by doing cool things utilizing the car or boat. Even if we were just chillin' on the boat, it was a welcome break from land for me and Luke always enjoyed being on the water. He's a Pisces.

November came around and I longed for St. John in ways that I hadn't imagined, but I never regretted my decision to leave. I began working as a barista on the weekends in a hospital cafeteria. I also worked a couple of nights as a cocktail server in a pool hall. I occasionally worked in a small, independent record store. Lastly, I worked for one month as an advertising salesperson, which is where I met one of my best friends, a writer named Badiyah. I gave our boss a copy of my zine to read. She got a hold of the copy and read it. Prior to, she didn't know much more about me than my name.

Badiyah loved my zine and couldn't wait to tell me, but wasn't sure how to tell me that she'd read it without my permission. She thought that I might be upset about it, but I wasn't at all. I felt honored and happy that she enjoyed it as much as she did, especially since she didn't really know me and she's a writer. She introduced me to Craig's list. She used to walk by and leave print outs of various job descriptions on my desk. I looked over them curiously. I was surprised and interested by many of the things she dropped off. I was so happy to have been exposed to such a wonderful resource. It was perfect for someone like me. I wish I knew of it sooner. Those feelings mirrored those that I had for Badiyah as well.

My birthday is on November 10th. That year, I woke up and cried from sadness within the first 15 minutes of my day. I felt so terrible in my situation. I was 28 years old. I had to go to work at a place I didn't really care to be, doing something I did not care to do, living with my grandmother whom I love dearly, but did not care to live with and Luke had told me the day before that his ex-girlfriend (the one he dated for 2 years before me) had just returned to St. John and that they might have sex that week. He didn't say it that easily, but I asked that bluntly. I wanted to be prepared. As much as I didn't want it to hurt so much, it did. I went to my mom's house that night and did my best to take it easy.

Laura, whose apartment I took over in St. John, was in Vermont feeling restless and talked about moving to Philly a few times, until one day she said it seriously. I was already looking for places to live to keep me sane while living with my grandmother. With Laura pitching in financially, I could find a place a lot faster, which made me excited. It was something to keep me going, for those were some long and challenging days.

Around my birthday, I had begun to let a large part of my romantic feelings for Luke go. It was ironic to me that 2 days later, on Friday, November 12th, a server from the Moshulu named Jean asked me out for a drink after our shift. He suggested that we meet up at a place ironically called "Luke's". If it wasn't so close to my grandmother's, I wouldn't have gone because I was pretty tired and don't drink often, especially in bars. Jean was nice, considerate, and pleasant though- with a French accent in a cute waiter uniform with wire rimmed glasses. His energy was different than everybody else's at the Moshulu too. That's the part I don't have the words to properly explain.

Over drinks we discussed art and philosophy, what we've done, doing and are going to do. My grandmother's building had a midnight curfew. I felt comfortable enough with Jean to stay at his place, so I asked him if it was okay with him if I stayed the night there, since he lived just 10 blocks or so from where I had to work at 6am the next morning. He had no problem with it. Over the next 5 weeks, I stayed there almost every day. We didn't kiss for almost a month. There was a strong attraction there, but I still felt put through the wringer emotionally in relation to Luke.

It was obvious that Jean had been through some wars himself, romantically speaking. He was kind and friendly enough, but still very guarded and distrustful. I did my best to wait a full month to kiss him, but one night, after being so turned on by just being around him, it was all over. We were pretty much together as a couple from then on. He had been casually dating 2 other women when we met, so I wasn't sure what he would end up doing now that feelings had developed between us.

By this time, Laura was planning on moving to Philly right after the New Year. I had just moved into our lovely new apartment 2 blocks away from 4th and South Sts. It wasn't a 2 bedroom, but it was large enough to make into a 2 bedroom. It was on the third floor of a house with roof access and two skylights. The rent was reasonable ($850/mo) and it was within walking distance of most major places in center city. The owner is a yogi. The place had wonderful energy inside. A week before Laura was to leave, she told me that she decided to stay in Vermont. The landlord had let me move in 2 weeks early because no one was there and I wanted to move right away. The rent was much more than I cared to pay by myself, but I did not feel like moving again, so I stayed.

I only had one full-time job as a barista at that point. I was offered a position as manager at a location not far from where I lived and close to Jean's place in west Philly. It's a big reason why I was at his place so much before I moved into my own. I enjoyed spending time with him, not being at my grandmother's and he was conveniently close to work. Jean had a roommate though, so once I moved into my place, it was PURE HEAVEN for me!!!

I started working 55-60 hours a week at the café sometime in December. I wanted the money. That persisted all winter long. It DUMPED snow on us 3 times that year too. I didn't even mind working that much. I would've been snowed in at home anyway. I thought, "It's better to make money while I'm stuck indoors." It was an easy gig- busy mainly in the mornings and slow to steady the rest of the day. I usually read magazines, sang along to music or chatted with the customers I befriended.

Around the end of February, I began to feel the itch to do something different. I felt I could find something else that offered comparable pay that was closer to my house. The best thing about being a barista there was that I made cash- anywhere from $35-$50 in a 10 hr day- on top of my salary. I also could eat whatever I wanted (not always a good thing) and drink whatever I wanted.

We hired someone to start around mid-February because I had no help and contracted the flu at one point and worked all day still. It was awful- the worst ever. The new person we hired, Lotus, I liked right away. She totally stood out from the other people I interviewed and I thought she'd be fantastic. She is. She's now one of my best friends. We kept in touch after I left the café. She and I were always busy, but we got together to record some music one day at my place. I built a small website for her using my new powerbook g4 laptop that someone from the café had recently given me.

One of our customers, Dan, had been telling me for months that he was going to give me a desktop computer because he wanted my help with a public service announcement that he was working on and he refurbished computers. We had talked over the months about our interests, so he knew that I was into film. He told me about all of the software he was going to install on the computer he was giving to me. As the date of my departure from the café neared, I wondered if he was really going to give me, what had now become, a laptop. I hadn't owned a computer since the laptop I owned while living on Alki died. I needed one badly, but couldn't afford it.

I think it was my last day at the cafe, when Dan brought in my brand new (refurbished), MacIntosh, Powerbook g4 laptop with Garage Band, Final Cut Pro, Illustrator, Photoshop and more. I knew that my life was forever changed. I had so much to learn!! With great tools come great responsibilities (to me) to use them well. I knew that Dan had all the faith in the world in me. I remember him mentioning a few times that it had garage band. I was most interested in using Final Cut Pro at the time. Dan and I have kept in touch since I left the café and are good friends still. I give him pieces of art as tokens of my appreciation.

The way Jean and I "officially" became monogamous was a sign of dangers to come. Jean had sex with one of the women that he was with before me sometime between Christmas and New Year's. I wasn't hurt that Jean had sex with the woman, but I was surprised. I asked him how he would feel if I had had sex with someone else and expected him to still be with me. He frankly said that he wouldn't go for it. That was that. We pretty much declared monogamy then because he didn't like the idea of me being with anyone else and I had pretty much given up on living within open, romantic relationships. I only cared to be with Jean at that point anyway.

Bill came to Philly for the holidays. His sister lived blocks away from my apartment. He invited me over to celebrate her birthday. When I first arrived, someone poured me a glass half full of vodka and the other half ginger ale. It was tasty and POTENT! I had a lot of fun dancing with everyone. We made dinner and smoked herb, took pictures and looked at ones already taken. I got sick in the bathroom shortly before I left (the alcohol and the herb mix). Bill walked me home. I remember some of the walk, going upstairs to say hi to Jean, then going back downstairs to say goodbye to Bill. I gave Bill a hug (I think) and then he kissed me.

I saw Bill in September, when I first got back from St. John, while still living with my brother. He was being a little flirtatious then, but sometimes that's just Bill. He and Alannah were still together and I didn't care to mess around with Bill like that anymore. I'm always flattered by his attention, but most times, not moved to do anything further. The times that I was, I didn't do a damn thing about it. I'd known the boy for 12 years. I was used to him. I didn't take him seriously in terms of romance or sex. I soon wished I took him very seriously, for that three-second kiss, which I do remember, was oddly enough, one of the most beautiful and wretched moments of my life.

It was a kiss out of the movies- a feeling of being suspended in mid air, like in a soap opera. Bill and I had a difficult time ending our sexual relationship for a reason. Our sexual chemistry was fantastic- better than we had expected. After enough time passes (like then and now), it's strange for me to think of past lovers, who've become friends, as lovers again. I did not expect that kiss. I expected a hug. If ANY thing, a closed mouth kiss, like we've given each other at times in the past, but not that. Bill was astonished and mortified afterwards upon realization that Alannah was arriving the next day to see him and meet his family and he had just kissed me.

He had to go back to his sister's. I told him to call me the next day. It wasn't a big deal to me then because I was so drunk and I hoped he wouldn't say anything, at least not right away. I didn't want anything bad to happen because of it. I knew it wasn't something that would keep happening. It felt like being sucked into a vortex of space and time. I hoped that he would decide to ignore that it happened and chalk it up to a drunken night. That's not how I'd normally deal with the situation, but this was a 3 second kiss between 2 people who'd shared many kisses and we were dealing with Alannah, who had serious trust issues, especially in relation to me. After Bill left, the last thing I remember is walking upstairs shaking my head in disbelief. How could life change so quickly in such dramatic ways in so short an amount of time?

The next morning at work, Bill called me around 6:30am. He was still up from the night before. Alannah was about to land in Chicago's airport en route to Philly. Bill planned to tell her what happened right away. I urged him to at least wait until she was in Philly to tell her in person. He didn't listen to me. He told her while she was in Chicago. She was furious at us both and hurt by both of us as well. She called me before I opened the cafe. I did my best to explain. I apologized and assured her that Bill and I have no unresolved feelings between us and that it was just a drunken night. I offered my apartment to them as a place they could be alone once she arrived in Philly for she didn't feel comfortable going to Bill's sister's right away.

I told Jean what happened after I finished work that day. He had met Bill before we met, before Bill moved to Seattle. Jean didn't care much for Bill then and that whole fiasco only made Jean like him less. It was an extremely difficult time for me because I adored Bill and had to accept the great rift between us that that kiss created. We used to be in much more frequent contact, even while I was in St. John. I understood that he needed time away from me due to all that had happened, but I didn't really get the severity of the situation. I was too wrapped up in all that was going on in my world.

Luke sent me a present for Christmas that year that I gave to my mom. It was a hook bracelet. They're commonly worn in the Caribbean. If the open end of the hook, which resembles a horse shoe and fastens the bracelet together, faces your fingers, it means you're available for romance, if it faces your body, you are not. The owner of Café Roma has a lovely daughter named Sarah. She gave me a small version of this bracelet (there are many styles) that I adore, with a piece of larimar (a blue stone that's from the Dominican Republic) set next to the hook.

The one that Luke sent to me, with a sweet note, was very beautiful. He rarely bought me things like that. It took my breath away and almost made me cry. It was the first I'd heard from him since my birthday. I was not happy about the fact that he basically ignored me the whole time since then. The bracelet was a nice gesture, but I didn't care to wear it. My mom always wanted one. She deserved it and was happy to have it. I told him that I gave it to her and I told her that he sent it to me. I waited to see what more he'd do, for I was fairly certain that he was still with his ex/current girlfriend. He was weird about taking my calls. He was erratic as to when he would call me back and/or text message me. Considering that I was happily involved with Jean, I was becoming very annoyed with his behavior.

Valentine's Day came around and Jean nor I planned to do anything special. He came to visit me at work on his way to work. He said that he would come by my place (15 min. walk from the Moshulu) after he was done. I showered, dressed overly sexy and cute, shoes and all, and fell asleep in a precise way so that I wouldn't be all disheveled once Jean arrived.

Why did I wake up at 2:45am and have NO missed calls, text messages or voicemails??? Where WAS my valentine/boyfriend? I called Jean and he was in a car on his way to a bar because he had a hard night at work- a "crazy table". Cops had to be called. It's expensive fine dining. It was only so "crazy". He didn't explain why he couldn't let me know anything the ENTIRE time. Mind you, the restaurant isn't open until 2am. Even with a fiasco, there was no good reason for him to have been there past 1am and to not have at least called. My boyfriend was justifying not coming to my place and seeing me on Valentine's Day because he wanted to go out with other people and drink.

That was the first time I broke up with Jean. I broke up with him 8 times over the course of the following 6 weeks. To Jean's credit, I met him during an emotionally depressed time during which I was smoking cigarettes (Nat Sherman MCDs) and drinking often (for me, say 2-3 times a week), not eating healthy and drinking coffee because it was free and I could have as much as I wanted.

Imbibing in all of the aforementioned were my ways of dealing with getting up so early in the morning, interacting with cranky office people and assembling the pieces of my broken heart, called my life. Several of my customers made my days. I keep in touch with some people from that place. One of my favorite things about working there was being able to play whatever music I wanted on the boom box. I used to sing along to Coldplay for WEEKS on end, after one of my awesome customers burned me their 2 cds. There was much happiness to explore and I was ready to reach out for it again. Coldplay helped remind me of this.

So the old saying, "It's not you, it's me." really fit in this case, with Jean as well as the cafe. I began to become healthy as the spring came and as I healed from my emotional wreckage. Jean had deep trust issues. I was good for him, as he was for me, for healing within our hearts to take place. He had a hard time believing my sincerity. He also didn't get that I had genuine male friends in my life that weren't just waiting around for their chance to have sex with me.

Jean's problem with men in my life was a big problem for me since I have about as many guy friends as I do girl friends. Seeing as I'm bisexual, it was ridiculous that this was such an issue to Jean in the first place. Any guy that called me annoyed him to no end. After 5 months, he still didn't trust me, which told me that he is not trustworthy. I find that most people who are trustworthy are more willing to know when others are worthy of their trust and to extend it. I knew that I was worthy, yet Jean wasn't extending. He was contracting, more and more after I had done all I could to show him that he could feel safe with me, at least enough not to cheat on him. Oddly enough, he trusted that it was Bill who kissed me and was upset with Bill, not me. However, that did happen within a few days of him having sex with someone else, so there was only so much he could say.

The final time we broke up, I had already left the café, quit cigarettes (his continual smoking, drinking and complaining about work wore on me) and began a new line of work- promotions. I looked forward to Jean having sex with another woman just for our affair to "officially" end. I thought that would do it. It is what did it, but he lied to me along the way, which created distance between us for about 5 months. I wasn't sure we'd ever be friends again.

He doesn't think he lied because to him, he wanted to tell me in person that he was having sex with someone new. I asked him on the phone one night because I sensed it. It had been about 2 weeks since we broke up. I asked him repeatedly if he'd been with someone else sexually and he wouldn't say anything at first. He just said that he wouldn't tell me regardless because he'd rather tell me something like that in person. I asked him to tell me anyway and he said that he hadn't been with anyone else sexually. I was skeptical, but believed him. The worst thing about a lie between people who are close is making that other person feel like they're feelings aren't congruent with the situation, like their intuition is off, when it's right on.

I was so fed up with Jean. I knew that he was upset by our breakup and he unleashed his anger in passive-aggressive ways. I was not happy that our exchanges had become so unpleasant. Those last 6-7 weeks we were together were so erratic. Things never escalated to violence, but both of our energies are so intense that it was very draining and exhausting for both of us. We knew we had to make some necessary changes, but not in the same ways and not together at that time.

Bill didn't contact me once since he returned to Seattle. I expected a couple of months to go by, but we were going on 4 months now without anything. I missed him and wanted to talk to him about all the bullshit going on with Jean and life in general. Bill was generally my guy friend that I shot the shit with about anything and everything, but especially relationships and Philadelphia.

When I contacted him, Bill was not in the mood to talk. Every thing that I sent via email during that time came across differently than I intended. He said that I sounded angry and pissed off. I was aiming to come across hurt, confused and pathetic (for I felt all of those things). I missed him like hell. I really wanted to talk to Bill. There was no substitute and it was as if he was dead, at least that "boyee" I had known and talked with so easily since high school. My faith in our friendship wavered for the first time ever.

It came out almost a year later (this past January) that he was angry at me for not being more understanding in regards to what he was going through and not being patient enough to ride out this tough period of our friendship. I wish he communicated with me more in some way. I was so used to feeling like Bill could say anything to me that no communication whatsoever was a very strange position for me to be in. The few conversations we did have, he wasn't sure what to say, but he kept mentioning how he felt I hadn't done enough to make Alannah feel better. Besides talking to her for a while the morning everything came out, I sent her an apologetic email right afterwards. I called later during her stay in Philly to do the same.

After Bill would say things like that, I'd email Alannah again to make sure everything was okay. Alannah seems to be more okay with all of this than Bill is at this point. I was disappointed that during this whole time, Bill seemed to care so little about how I was doing or how I felt. I know he fucked up with his girlfriend whom he loves. I am a woman he's known almost half his life whom he fucked up with too and yet, I get this angry, "How can you not understand??" voice instead of bothering to explain a damn thing to me as to what is going on. How was I supposed to know how serious this all is/was if he doesn't tell me shit?! Shit…

My main concern was my friendship with Bill, for I wasn't that close to Alannah. We used to be closer, like when we were emailing before she returned to Seattle right before we were all about to leave for St. John. I'd made more efforts due to her deep involvement with Ariana and Bill. Alannah's distrust and lack of openness was something I didn't feel like "working on". I had "worked enough" with friends that I had brought into my life over the years. She was not an easy person for me to feel close to within city limits, let alone long distance.

Before I left for St. John, I made efforts to spend time with Alannah and to talk to her on the phone and it generally didn't happen. I was tired of being disappointed by her. I wasn't as enamored with her as Ariana and Bill were, so my patience with her was much thinner, especially during those times. Alannah is a cool woman, who has inspired me since her teenage years, but I appreciated her then more on a parallel plane, not so much on a closely intertwining one. I think Ariana and Bill took personal offense to my change of feelings towards Alannah, in ways. After Bill kissed me, it became evident that my relationship with the three of them had changed dramatically.

Ariana, one of my closest friends who had known me for almost a decade questioned my feelings towards Bill, which I'd been upfront about always, with everyone. This was a result of skepticism on her behalf, Alannah's and/or Bill's. We almost got into one of few fights between us because she kept pushing the issue of me looking deeper at my feelings for Bill, which I had willingly done so on numerous occasions, yet Bill's attraction towards me was easily glazed over. I assured them all that us kissing would not happen again. To ensure that, all I have to do is not drink a lot around Bill so that I'm not susceptible to any advances, for that's the only time I could see it ever possibly happening again and it's not because I secretly want it to; it's because I don't drink often, am a "lightweight" and alcohol can severely impair judgment. I'm so comfortable with Bill and I have kissed him so many times that I can not say that I'd never kiss him again. It's not something I think about doing though, not even when we were sexually involved. It was more like something good that happened that kept happening that we knew had to stop eventually.

It took me until November of last year (almost a year later) to get to the point where I could talk to Bill without feeling resentful, angry or hurt by the way he treated me throughout '05. The real heart to heart conversation we had over the phone in January '06 is where we got a lot of things out. We haven't talked much since then. Better times are in the future between us, I hope. As I've mentioned before, sometimes, even I still have a hard time letting go of old ways and embracing change. I don't always like it, but I work to always accept it and do the best I can with what I have.

At the end of March ('05), I met 2 women named Jets and Melanie and 1 man named Larry, who was our manager, while working my first promotion for three weeks. I'm still good friends with them to this day. Badiyah, from the advertising place, worked with us for a few days too. It was the first time I saw Badiyah in months. She knew Melanie from when they took a class together. We all got along wonderfully, which helped work feel less like work..

Lotus is one with whom I feel a strong connection with when as well. She's what you would call a "girl's girl" (her term), in that she's all about "the empowered female" and women being there to support each other, not bring each other down. During my last days at the café, Lotus mentioned that her friend Reese had been in contact with a woman who was a Tina Turner impersonator and that she needed dancers. Reese is a choreographer.

Lotus brought up the Tina Turner show again a couple of months later after actually meeting with the woman. I met with them all and had a few rehearsals before backing out. It was too much time and money going out and not enough coming in for me to keep attending. We had rehearsal once a week in New Jersey, with more closer to the first performance. We would be paid per performance, but I wasn't willing to commit seeing as I needed to work and make money- and lots of it- as soon as possible.

I wanted to leave myself open to working as many promotions as I could in order to build more experience and get more work for I found the work to be easy, at times, fun and it paid well. At some point in April, I'd taken a part-time job as a receptionist in a chiropractor's office up the street from me. She hadn't been practicing long. She was a fairly nice woman and terrific doctor. She was certified as a nutritionist too. I walked out of her office one day (I left a long note of explanation) after she took a tone with me that was completely unnecessary. I had sacrificed too much of myself to be there for that sort of treatment, even for a second. It was harsh and I really wasn't in the mood that day.

Lani is Devon's sister who lived in Philadelphia during the time that I moved here from St. John. We hung out with Devon at her place when he came to visit that fall. We got along so well that we kept in touch over the winter, meeting up for coffee and occasional nights, drinking wine, chit-chatting about our lackluster boyfriends whom we loved, while wishing for more out of life, in general. She was my main and closest friend during my first six months back in Philly.

Lani was the first person I called after I left the chiropractor's office. She abhorred jobs that made one feel unappreciated just as much as I did. Lani used to dream of moving to Asheville, NC since she visited Devon, who had been living there for a few years. In June, she and her boyfriend packed up their house and business, moved out of Northern Liberties and into the Smoky Mountains. I miss Lani dearly. I visited for four days in August, right after she left. I wish she lived closer.

My apartment by 4th and South St. was $850/mo. After I quit the café, it became an overwhelming amount to come up with (plus utilities) every month. I began to resent my beautiful place. One night, I met up with Lotus and Reese at Lotus' apartment to rehearse for the Tina show. Lotus told me about her place when I first hired her. I wondered why she lived in Mt. Airy when she worked in the city all the time (she was a personal trainer as well). I soon realized why. Her apartment was only $500/mo for a big one bedroom with a full-size kitchen, basement, front porch, back porch and yard.

The apartment was ridiculously nice, roomy and had a homey feel to it because it's on the first floor of a twin house. I felt myself falling in love every moment I was there. Lotus had mentioned moving to Los Angeles a few times, but hadn't set anything in stone. She was unsure when she would have enough money saved to go. Her tentative plan was to leave in the fall. I told her that I would love to have her apartment once she moved.

Due to my rent being so high and promotions being unpredictable, I asked Lotus to consider the idea of me living with her until she moved to L.A., in order for us both to save money and for her to be more motivated to actually do it (she'd been thinking about it for 5 years). It was easy for me to move my things in because I had the basement to store things in throughout the transition.

My brother and 2 nephews moved in with my mom once my brother sold his house in preparation for his move to North Carolina. They moved in with my mom some time in July '05. He moved his living room furniture into Lotus' place before I moved in on August 1st. I moved into a wonderfully decorated and comfortably furnished humble abode. I was so tired of moving. Lotus kept mentioning the possibility of me moving to L.A. I thought that I'd go eventually, but it most certainly was not the time for me to seriously think about it. It was a big stress relief to see myself staying in one place for a while.

My landlady from my center city place spoke with the owner. They were kind enough to end my 12-month lease after 7 months, without deducting one penny from my deposit. They were very gracious and fair people with whom I was quite pleased with as a tenant. The same woman lives in the neighborhood right next to mine, Chestnut Hill, which I love as well.

The twins' stepbrother, Tom (we all hung out in high school. He's 4 years older than us) lived several blocks from my center city place. We ran into each other shortly after I moved in December of '04. We kept in touch, visiting each other about once a month. In May, Tom found out that his apartment building was about to undergo serious renovations and that he had to find a new place within 30 days. I offered to let him stay with me (which he did) to extend his time in order not to feel pressured into a less than satisfactory place. Unfortunately, he ended up taking a place that was decent, but the landlord was AWFUL!

Thankfully, he was only in that place for 6 weeks ('twas 6 weeks too many- according to him!). He stayed with me from mid-June until the end of July, when I moved to Mt Airy. It began as a two-week stay, but I had a feeling it would be longer. Things happen. Tom's always been respectful, nice and fair to me. I did not mind helping him out whatsoever. A few times were a challenge due to our friends and miscommunications, but we worked everything out fairly quickly and easily. We're both honest people, which helped a LOT!

I was happy to move in with Lotus, another very honest person who only became more trusting of me over time. Conversations flow in more entertaining, insightful and thought-provoking ways, I find, when I'm having an open discussion with someone who isn't guarded with their thoughts and/or feelings in regards to any matter. I'm not looking for anyone to be that way all the time. It is fantastic when I come across people who allow themselves to at least be that way with me though. This is where Lotus and I connect, as well as many other areas. We both love music- listening to it, singing it, dancing to it, playing guitar to it (I eventually taught myself to play on the guitar that her father gave to her), writing it, recording it and watching people perform it, among other things, I'm sure. Living together was easier than either of us thought it would be.

Lotus and I both love movies, but professionally, music is our first love. For a while, I thought that acting was Lotus' main pull to move to L.A. She would act, but performing music is her main goal. It's funny that we were brought together in the ways that we were and have kept in touch, for completely different reasons other than our music. We're extremely encouraging and supportive of one another's music and career choices along the unknown paths of our lives as artists in the new millennium. I don't think either of us ever takes the other for granted.

As scary as it may seem at times, we both feel very sure of what we're doing. Some things have happened in both of our lives better than we could have planned. We struggle, but aren't deterred by our struggles. We are thankful when they're over, do our best to prevent them and share what we learn along the way so that others might avoid our errors. I would say that most of the women in my life (family included) echo these feelings.

In July, I called Jean about a couple of paintings and his things that I had for him to take before I moved. He came and got them, but we didn't see each other. We had a couple of decent phone exchanges. We texted pleasantly, then finally saw each other at some point in August. Slowly, but surely, our relationship has progressed to a healthy, functional friendship. It was questionable at times, but it's remained steady for a bit now. It seems to be on course. We each have our moments, but they're much easier to rectify.

Last year around April or May, I mailed out a bunch of letters to people I hadn't spoken to in a while after coming across some old letters and address books. One of the people I sent a letter to was Raphael. He called me within a week. The only address I had for him was his aunt's house in Argentina. She told him of its arrival. He asked her to open it and read to him the numbers that were there. She read him my phone number. He called me right away and we talked for the first time in 3 years. It was nice to hear him so happy to talk to me. I wasn't expecting that. I didn't remember what I'd said in my letter, but it didn't matter because he never read it!

Our conversation flowed very easily, unlike the last time I spoke with him. He could barely speak to me then. He's been living in Miami for a few years as a full-time artist. I was very proud to hear of his accomplishments for I am inspired by "real life success stories", especially of those I know (and to whom I was married). We've kept in touch way more than I had expected since then. I'll elaborate more on Raphael shortly.

In June, I interviewed for a position as a barista at a brand new café set to open the first week of July within walking distance of my new place in Mt. Airy. The promotions field was lucrative, but not steady enough to ensure I'd be able to pay my rent, so I accepted the position at the cafe. The commute for the first 3 weeks was the PITS!! It took a minimum of an hour and a half to get to the café from my center city place. The café owner understood most times, but towards the end, I called crying one morning because I was running late and felt so bad about it. I wasn't used to the train schedule or getting up so early. It was a nightmare. I was really looking forward to finally living in Mt. Airy.

It's been a dream come true. When I first hung out in this area during my high school years, I had a hard time believing that I was still in Philadelphia. It was so close to my house, yet I never knew about it. I didn't get why my brother or my mother had never brought me here before in my life! I loved it so much here then and love it even more now that it's become gay friendly and even more community oriented. There are tee shirts I see that read, "I like Mt. Airy". Mine will have "like" crossed out and over it will read "LOVE"! It's one of the most integrated areas/neighborhoods in any major city in the United States. I see people who look like me (of mixed ethnicity) all over this area.

There are lots of trees around and a beautiful section of Fairmount Park, which is the largest park within city limits in the U.S. It was designed by the Olmsted Brothers, whose firm was well known for designing Central Park as well as most parks in and around Seattle. Valley Green (the section of Fairmount near here) is within walking and biking distance. Shops and markets, video stores and friends, trains and buses are minutes away. These are just some of the main reasons why I've fallen in love with Philadelphia this time around, in ways I had never even imagined.

Manhattan still holds a special place in my heart, however, when I worked there for three weeks in midtown last September ('05) while staying at Henry's house in Brooklyn, I came home every weekend because I missed my place in Mt. Airy DEARLY!! I missed the smell of the trees the most. The stench of the subways in the summertime was a new experience that I had the pleasure of missing when I lived in Manhattan years before. I would rather not revisit that experience ever again.

I threw Lotus a going away party at the end of that September, right before she left, and invited all of her friends. A few of mine that live around here came by for a bit, including a guy named Ty whom I had worked with once at the café during my last day, which was right before the party. Ty was one of my replacements. The cafe simply wasn't for me. I was doing a pretty good job finding enough promotional work to keep me afloat. The 3-week gig in Manhattan helped a lot too. I also filed back taxes from the previous 2 years, due to Lani's prompting, and got back almost $2,000, which came at a perfect time for I had major bills to catch up on from my old place. The majority of that money came from working at Pegasus. That manager was so awesome.

The night of Lotus' going away party, I fell asleep on the floor in Ty's arms (several people stayed the night). When I woke up in them the next morning, I kissed him. I'm not even sure why. I think because he was so adorable. He was sweet and funny too. I liked that a lot. He was good looking, kind of shy, but not too shy. He was environmentally conscious about his choices, which I loved. He began to help out in my life as much as he could. He helped Lotus too. We began spending a ton of time together because he lived so close and we were kissing more and more. I did my best to stop after the first time, but it was so easy to fall into after that first time- the morning after the party. He was such a good kisser too.

A little more than a month later (I was aiming to wait at least 3 months), we had sex. He was so shy. I wasn't used to that. I wasn't sure how to respond. I decided to talk openly with him and not make him feel pressured to do anything at anytime. He was placing unnecessary expectations on himself and it resulted in discordance between us for I could tell when he was trying too hard versus going with the flow. Talking about things honestly helped him to relax and enjoy himself, which made me enjoy myself and a happy relationship was born.

However, as time went on (remember Lesson #1??), I learned more about Ty's character. I watched and listened to the things he said and did. I saw who he was working towards being and I believed in that, but that's not who I was with, even though it's who I preferred to be with- his ideal self. I was aware of that fact, but I wasn't interested in being sexual with anyone else, yet. We had a very good sexual relationship for one month. It's one of few times I was with someone romantically and didn't feel like we'd be together indefinitely. I knew that at some point along the way, we'd break up. Most times, once I become aware of that fact, it's over.

What broke us up "technically" was when he told me that a family friend of his mom's, named Roe and her daughter, Doris (who just so HAPPENS to be one of the twins'-Tim- ex-girlfriend from before we lived together and got it on) were over Ty's mom's house (where Ty lived while his mom was living on the West Coast) one day while Ty's

mom was home visiting for Thanksgiving. At some point I came up.
I forewarned Ty that Doris might have shit to say because of Tim. Roe
and Doris talked shit about me and Ty told me that his younger sister
and brother, stood up for my character and said that they didn't know me
well, but perhaps I had changed in 10 years for I seemed like a really
nice person now.

Ty told me that he just sat there the entire time hiding behind his
cat, being a pussy alongside him. This was a man who said that he loved
me and that I meant the world to him. I've been there myself. I know
what it feels like to allow others to desecrate things you hold sacred-
with their words and/or actions. I would do my best to never allow that
to happen these days. It made any attraction for Ty that I had vanish.
That incident happened around Thanksgiving. Ty and I weren't seeing
much of each other those days anyway due to all the time I was spending
at work on my first feature film. Therefore, it wasn't that hard to let him
go.

October was a slow month for work. I took that time to get my
new place in order. I began training one of Lotus' clients who didn't
have another personal trainer. She's the only client I have and probably
will have. We've been working out pretty much every week since
October '05. She's an inspiring woman that I look forward to meeting
up with every week. She is 56, had never exercised before 2 years ago,
has lost over 200 pounds, and does her best to eat primarily vegetarian
and exercise 4-5 times a week. Training her has been one of the best
regular things in my life this past year.

On Craig's list, in October, I came across an ad for positions for
crew in a feature film ("The UnGodly") being shot in and around
Philadelphia for 5 weeks in November. It was a MIRACLE that I
actually got the position as "crafty" (Craft Services~ supplying snacks,
drinks, gum, pb & j, etc.) to all cast and crew throughout the shoot. I had
never done craft services before. I was supposed to have a car, I didn't.
Someone I was going to work with (I asked her because her schedule
was open and she had a car) ended up having too much attitude for me,
so I got out of her car in the middle of traffic and screamed, "There is
NO WAY I am going to work 12 hours a day, 6 days a week over the
next 5 weeks with you!!" and walked away, 4 days before shooting
began. Lo and behold, another miracle.

Jim (yup, one of the twins) was living around here and I hadn't
seen him in months. A day or 2 after I had no partner anymore, I ran into
Jim and his boyfriend Hank around the corner at a local hangout. I

proposed the idea to them, desperately looking for someone cool with a car, just so I could still work the gig. The production company offered $100 flat rate for the day. I would've been happy with $75/day just to work on a film set. It was a small company, but professional. Fortunately, Hank wasn't happy at his job as a server anyway and took a leave of absence. I was thrilled! They ended up using his car in the movie, so he got paid even more than he thought he would, which was awesome.

Those 5 weeks were grueling at times, for it only got colder as the shoot went on. However, many of those days were the most fun I've ever had at work, largely thanks to Hank. We laughed a lot! It was insane, especially towards the end when most people were so ready to wrap. Many of the execs were from Los Angeles, so they weren't used to Philly weather in December (The movie wrapped on December 6th). Our winter was setting in and it was wearing away at all of us. Hank and I took good care of our people. They loved us both in our own way. We did our very best to accommodate everyone's needs.

The second or third day of the shoot was my birthday. We were filming at at one of the producer's house and he found out that it was my birthday that morning. He kept mentioning it to various people throughout the day, like when they walked by while we were talking or something. We worked 12-16 hour days, 6 days a week, so I only made plans (sometimes) on Sundays, our day off. I would usually use the phone while working. Since Lani is one of my best friends, and her birthday had just passed 3 days before mine AND it had been a while since I'd talked to her, I was especially happy when I got through to her and we had some time to talk!

Within 5 minutes of our conversation, Hank called me to meet him inside the house where they were shooting. I was a little annoyed because he didn't even know why we were needed. A minute later, someone had come out to find me to bring me in to see my boss- the man who gave me money and to whom I gave receipts. I was nervous because I had spent their first $200 and had given him the receipts for my purchases just a couple of hours ago. I thought I'd screwed up somehow.

My boss called me over and loudly proclaimed to me that he had $4 that he owed me. Then he yelled to a producer asking for $2 more for me. I was thoroughly embarrassed at this point because I thought that they would all think I was harassing the poor man for $6. That's when I turned around and saw the producer, who had wished me a happy birthday throughout the whole day, with a cheesecake in his hand full of candles on top and everyone all around me began singing "Happy Birthday" to me.

I went from feeling nervous, to embarrassed, to overjoyed and finally grateful (for the job, people and love) in such a short span. I wept like a baby (PMS- I was emotional). I had never had that happen before in front of that many people. The energy I felt coming from everyone was so strong that it's all I could do. I couldn't stop crying. I cried the entire song through, doing my best to keep breathing. 4 people sang a Hebrew birthday song immediately afterwards as well. It was one of the most amazing and touching experiences I've ever had with strangers. I still keep in touch with some of those people. Filmmaking can be quite a bonding experience.

In October, I set up a job for the month of December, doing the lighting and sound for a Christmas show in King of Prussia. It was a 2-hour commute, but I didn't care because my job made me feel like the "Wizard" from "The Wizard of Oz", in a positive way. I had a lot of fun there. It was pretty easy, but there were too few patrons for them to keep me on payroll, so I was let go for the last 10 days of the run, which really sucked because I had already gone Christmas shopping before knowing I was going to be out $700 and it was right before rent was due.

The holidays came. Devon visited my new place for the first time on Christmas Eve. He stayed the night here before his girlfriend arrived from Rhode Island on Christmas. We drank alcohol together with no problem at all, just a few beers each. He helped me wrap presents. It was peaceful and lovely. I went to mom's house the next day and had a good ol' time hanging out with the kids and my brother all day on Christmas.

That's basically what I did for New Year's Eve too. I happened to have a can of black eyed peas at home already (rare), so I bought a can of greens (I wasn't as into cooking from scratch again yet) and put them both on the stove for good luck in the New Year. It was the second year ever (not in a row) that I followed the southern tradition that many in my family follow religiously. Kelly (my youngest nephew) and Jahdiera (my niece) stayed at my place the whole weekend.

My mom and brother were invited as well, but they made other plans. We watched the ball drop on television and toasted our sparking apple juice. I was so happy to have them in my place, in my world and in my heart. It was a perfect way for me to bring in my new year. The previous year, mom and I were on the Moshulu. I got back to her with two glasses of champagne as soon as the countdown reached, "One!"

and the fireworks went off (long line for champagne). It was a spectacular moment. We both love fireworks and hadn't spent New Year's Eve together in a very long time.

January is typically a slow month for promotions, but I at least had one that I worked somewhat regularly that offered good pay with minimal hours. One very good thing that came from the ample time I had all of a sudden (once I was let go) was my lifestyle change. I began to eat better because I had more time to cook. I began to dance and sing, stretch and practice yoga, chant and/or meditate more and more.

In August, a man that I met in a café (where he worked) a couple of blocks from my house asked me if it was okay to offer my niece some fruit since she was playing with his daughter in the back of the café. I had no problem with that. We exchanged phone numbers. One of the first things that he mentioned to me upon first talking to me outside of the café was that he's a practicing Nichiren Buddhist.

I had learned about the chant "nam myoho renge kyo" (one translation: I devote myself to the law of cause and effect) just a few months prior to meeting this man named Miles. I'd been curious about Buddhism for years. I had read numerous books on it, but I'd never met a practicing Buddhist who was openly willing to share their practice with me, so I listened to what Miles had to share. I attended evening gongyo, but time constraints, especially that involve me leaving my house, can be very difficult for me. I chant almost every day still (I've had lulls since August) usually after I practice yoga and meditate. I tend to conclude everything (yoga and chanting, sometimes quiet meditation sessions) by chanting "Om" three to seven times.

Miles is an interesting character. He's a talented artist, like many of my friends. He is young and still discovering his voice. I've heard him play guitar and tear it up! He has a passion for the trumpet and Miles Davis, but lately, his main expression has been painting. He's melding the 2 together, working on his expression of music using the visual arts as his medium. One of the most wonderful things about hanging out with Miles is that it's easy to hang out with each other while we do our own things artistically. He'll paint or draw while I work on whatever I'm into at that time.

With nicer weather upon us, I've been taking more of my friends for walks around the neighborhood and through the woods and going biking all around. One of my friends, Rob, who lives 3 blocks away, has been Bill's best friend for over half of his life and was Bill's roommate for 5 or 6 years when they lived in center city. Rob's like a brother to me. He lets me use his washer and dryer for my laundry since that's the one thing my place doesn't have. His place is much better than going to a laundromat!! He's a cook at the local hang out around the corner, where I ran into Jim and Hank. This is the neighborhood where he grew up, so sometimes he's a bit tired of it, then we go for a bike ride through Valley Green and he remembers one of the reasons why he's called this place home for so many years.

Maxine's old house (from high school) is in my neighborhood. It was hard not to think about her while here. I worked Live 8 last summer and saw her backstage, from 4 feet away, yet I said nothing. I didn't care to witness her discomfort. There was a guitarist that I'd known to be a part of Maxine's circle of friends. I made contact with him and hung out with him a few times shortly after I moved to Mt. Airy. One day I came across Maxine's profile on myspace. I decided to contact her once again, for I'd sent her 3 emails over 3 years with no response. I didn't want there to be any awkwardness or tension if we ran into each other at a show or something.

When Maxine and I were in Spain, she introduced me to Kayla, whom I adore! I've kept in touch with Kayla pretty well over the years. She came to visit us both in 2001, but she wasn't feeling well for most of that trip, unfortunately. It was good to see her anyway. Kayla and her boyfriend came to visit us again last March ('05). It was tough for Kayla, for Maxine and I hadn't spoken in three years. O yeah, I forgot to mention that Maxine stopped talking to me in the spring of '03.

During the time when I was broke in Seattle, the time when I considered selling my body for sex, Maxine's first cd had been released. I was very supportive of her, but couldn't afford to buy the cd. I had spent everything I had on publishing my zine and feverishly looked for worthwhile work. Maxine had more money than me (up to that point) for most of her life. I had always been more materially generous with her than she was with me (she admitted that) and I was tired of her selfish behavior.

The fact that I wasn't a close enough friend to her for her to freely share her music, upset me, especially considering how poor I was at that time and how much I love music. It's very inexpensive to burn a cd. She had given me a website of where to purchase it. All I wanted was to hear the first cd that one of my best friend's created. I couldn't afford it and to ask for it for free showed a lack of support on my end, according to her.

We went back and forth via letters and emails until she cut me out of her life by asking me to contact her no further. This was after I had said that I didn't see our dialogue progressing and suggested taking a step back, as a breather. I didn't think she would react like that. I hurt her beyond repair in confronting her about things I'd kept to myself in regards to her and materialism. There were a few incidents of her being overly thrifty and me being overly generous that I showcased in my writings. The whole ordeal with the cd is what made me finally say something. I never did before because I didn't want to make her feel uncomfortable, but I'd grown tired of this sort of treatment by someone to whom I would have given the shirt off of my back. My words weren't malicious or spiteful. They were factual. Sometimes the truth hurts. That's life.

Maxine and I had a very good heart to heart when we first met up in the beginning of this year and it's funny to me that she didn't even remember the cd as being the catalyst for us not talking. She had simply held onto the fact that I had severely hurt her and that I was a "toxic relationship" to her. She threw away most of the things I'd given her when she moved into her new house last fall with her husband whom she married a little more than a year ago.

Talking about Maxine's husband is one of the main reasons she's not talking to me again, which began a few months ago. Our "reunion" was short-lived. I won't get into details for I have a feeling that somehow these words will cross her path and I don't care to make her feel any worse about herself because of what I choose to share here. To voice my opinions completely as to why we're not speaking now doesn't feel like the best idea.

I don't enjoy being a source of pain to anyone. I respect Maxine for what she strives for from her heart and for her love and reverence towards music and spirituality. I don't think that she'll be out of my life forever and I'll welcome her back. I have learned more and more that "birds of a feather DO flock together" and "opposites do attract" (and oftentimes are/become co-dependent). Both are true!! O life's paradoxes.

Fortunately for me during the brief period that things were going well between us she invited me to her birthday party at her home shortly after we began speaking again. It's where I met a very good friend and hip-hop/rap artist named Kwame Andah from Ghana. Since it was the first time I'd hung out with Maxine in a group setting, I was a bit nervous about being in her home amongst her closest friends after such estranged times. Kwame and I hit it off immediately. I loved his energy, intelligence, kind heart and spirit. We have more in common than we ever imagined upon first meeting. Ironically enough, he knew Nina too, who was at the party and was someone I hadn't seen in a years. She's a singer as well.

Nina is a friend of Maxine's that is 6 years younger than she. Nina and I used to talk a lot when she stopped talking to me 3 and a half years ago because I was more honest with her than she cared for me to be. She was at Maxine's birthday party in January of this past year. That was the first time I'd seen her since the summer before I left for Seattle the last time, in '02. We got along fine for the brief time we interacted with each other. We hung out shortly after Maxine's party.

I thought Nina had changed in ways where we could get along harmoniously. I wasn't upset when she stopped talking to me before, which happened because she wasn't pleased with me saying that I didn't believe she was really in love with her boyfriend. It was obvious, I thought. I was mistaken. Nina stopped talking to me again three months later, a week before her birthday, due to some things that transpired in relation to Miles. She wasn't happy with the level of honesty I shared with him or her.

I do lie at times. Rarely is it premeditated. It usually happens if I feel put on the spot about something that makes me feel uncomfortable in that moment. I think about it a lot afterwards too in order to learn from it because I prefer to be 100% honest all the time. I wasn't happy with Nina's level of honesty, but I was still willing to be her friend. I have no problem with her choice not to be mine. I can be very difficult for some to be close with as a friend. People, places and feelings (and more) all change. Why get my panties in a bunch each time? My tattoo being on my back represents change itself, for even though I don't see it (without a mirror. Haha!! True in both cases), it's always there.

Nina at one point was considering living with Badiyah, which I could not see. They'd drive each other mental. Nina is way too rigid for Badiyah who's more free-spirited, spontaneous and relaxed about life. Nina was looking for a place to live much sooner than Badiyah anyway. Funny to picture the two of them living together. Glad that never happened. I'm sure that they are too!

Badiyah and I understand each other on a level that few others do. We are artistic, entrepreneurial women that do our best to bend life to our rules, instead of the other way around, and do surprisingly well at this, sometimes, insurmountable task. We were this way before we met each other and continue to be so now. We keep each other going. Her writings, conversations and funky styles inspire me and vice/versa. We constantly bounce new ideas off of one another and give each other useful feedback in critical ways that are constructive, without tearing our feelings apart destructively.

On January 13th, 2006, I had my first real flutters of a burgeoning Internet romance. I never dated online. I never signed up for any dating services or anything of the sort. This came as a complete surprise to me. We met on myspace. Her profile was very flirtatious, just like her. I didn't expect anything serious to become of it at all. She was a singer/songwriter with a love for life that paralleled my own, which was clearly shown all over her page.

The object of my affections lived in Slovenia. She was a journalist as well and enchanted me with her words and photos. Within one week, I had professed my love to her, Eva, and the whole world (all my family and friends). It was all so new to me, yet I didn't doubt its validity because of the strength of my feelings. I was on a natural high that made me feel like I was queen of the universe! Everyone that I told in person and on the phone knew that the love I felt was real. I'm not a cheater though, so I confronted Eva about some things that I was unsure of, seeing how strong our feelings had grown in such a short amount of time.

That night I asked for more details about the woman she was going to visit in Los Angeles in 3 weeks. She told me early on that they'd never met, but they'd been in touch over 8 or 9 months. She wasn't totally sure about being with her. She was a journalist and had an assignment during her stay. She flirted with me and bared much of her soul to me (family history, hopes, fears, friends) via emails, instant messages, web cam, photos (very sexy, no nudes) and two long phone conversations over the course of 2-3 weeks.

In the very beginning I asked her if I had a chance of really being with her, for I wanted to know before allowing any emotions to grow. I was already surprised by what was there through all that we had in common and a few synchronistic events. If you received those emails and photos (the FIRST one was of her in a bikini in the middle of a lake looking seductively into the camera while biting her knuckle, ever so gently) you would've been tempted too! Then she told me the name of the woman she intended to see and I saw her profile and found out that according to her, Eva was her girlfriend.

I felt terrible. I was "the other woman". Shit! How did that happen? Things had to shift, but I so wish they hadn't even gone as far as they did. I emailed Eva right away saying that we cannot instant message anymore and that she was not to call me anymore either, not until she decided what she was going to do. She called me that night saying that she felt she had to call, no real explanation, she just had to talk to me. We had a very strong connection that I do not deny, but I didn't want to be the cause of her breakup with the woman she had been in touch with for 8 or 9 months, hadn't even met yet and was about to fly to see! She called herself "Miss Crazy". I didn't heed the warning.

The first few days were okay. I was communicating with her best friend (a gay male dancer) to alleviate the longing that I felt due to her sudden absence. We saw each other on instant messenger and gave in several times. It was tough to keep our feelings purely platonic. Our caring and attraction came out through our words, especially considering we're both writers. I sent her the first part of what I wrote of this book, when it was a zine. She knew that I'd told just about everyone in my life about her, for I was planning a trip to Europe! She encouraged me to go. She seemed so sweet. It made me remember why some find me so unbelievable. I was hoping that she'd come visit me for Valentine's Day. She said that she was going to tell Destiny, her girlfriend, about me "eyeball to eyeball". I trusted that she would at least tell her that I was a good friend.

It became obvious to me where I stood, when just 3 weeks later, she was preparing to leave and I asked her to call me when she could from L.A. She made it clear that it would pretty much be impossible, which I thought was strange considering she told me that she was going to tell Destiny about me no matter what she decided. That was my first clue that she was a liar. She didn't make her whole life up or anything. She simply isn't straight with people all the time. I didn't want that, but I did want some of what we had. When close friends of mine saw her profile, they understood our connection, which only skimmed the surface. I'm not one to do natal chart comparisons, but for her, I did.

Once Eva returned from L.A., I thought that we could at least be friends- as cool as we were before, but not as intimate. Eva was cold and barely paid me the time of day. This was from a woman who said that I could buy a ticket to see her in Europe (to spend time with her AFTER she returned) before she left for L.A. Yes, her feelings might have changed while she was there, but what if I had actually gotten the ticket by that time? I understand committing yourself to someone, but to turn your back completely on someone who opened themselves to you and vice/versa without any explanation was unexpected, to say the least.

Realizing that Eva might do this again and that I'd want to know if I was in Destiny's place, I emailed Eva's girlfriend an email from the beginning, middle and end of our correspondence so she could see the progression of our relationship. I included pictures Eva had sent as well. Eva told Destiny that I lied, but the proof was in the pudding, so I thought. Eva was a better liar than I gave her credit for! There was no way I could know certain words that only she used. At one point, Destiny asked me to call her, but I didn't want to get that involved.

The most ironic thing is that now Destiny and I are friends. She contacted me a couple of months later after catching Eva being shady and wanted to clarify once and for all what really happened. I told her everything, this time in full detail. Eva and I haven't been in contact since the first time I told Destiny everything. Eva had the nerve to call me a bitch. Destiny is a kind, compassionate and loving person whom I am very happy to have gotten to know. I never thought we'd be friends as a result of all that has happened. At least something positive has come out of this whole fiasco. It can be a struggle to find genuine people anywhere. It's always nice to come across a kindred spirit.

My friend Kevin, who was a fellow manager at the café I used to manage, whom I'd never met until my last days there because we worked at two different locations is one of these people. We became friends instantaneously. I heard enough about him to know that we would get along well. On a cold winter night, he gave me a thick lounge/bath robe that he no longer used because it was cold outside and he wanted me to have it to wear home. This was after he had me over and made dinner for his roommates and me. I am not a "fashionista" and cold weather is a tough one for me to contend with, so I walked through the streets of center city in my newly acquired bathrobe, thanking Kevin for my new gift that I'd wanted for a while. That was the first night we hung out.

I've been grateful for the robe and Kevin ever since. It was a very gracious gesture, quite indicative of him, as well as others who have given me things; like Byron, who gave me a fantastic 3 disc stereo or Eddie who has dedicated numerous hours towards the advancement of my video and musical knowledge. Byron has taken my niece, my nephew, his daughters and me to the Jersey shore. Eddie helped me put together an audition tape for MTV to have my own reality show. 2 minutes of footage took us about 6-8hours of time. That's video! I love it and thankfully Eddie does too and is so willing to help me and show me things for free. My camcorder died while sailing in St. John. I look forward to owning another one and exploring this passion once again.

Dan (who gave me this laptop that is allowing me to type up this book) took Kelly, Jahdiera and me to a horse show last summer where I took this postcard picture of the 3 of us. It was a chilly day. I was very tired and felt like napping all day, but my niece loves horses. Kelly just came because he was with us. Dan and his sister were in the show. I'd never been to a horse show before. I took some photos with Dan's camera as well as my own. I love simply using iphoto to doctor images. Mac Intosh has become my new boyfriend. He's still one of the best ever "tangibles". Music is up at the top of the "intangibles" list.

Let me state here and now that even though I just listed a bunch of things that men in my life have given me, my female friends have been JUST as awesome in every which way. They've been mentioned all throughout this book. They are generous with their material things too. Men simply don't generally allow me to get as emotionally close to them as I do my girl friends unless they are having sex –or think they're going to- have sex with me. That being said, my guy friends are honest and trustworthy and are really my true friends, thus the generosity and consistency in my life. We all have different ways of expressing emotions. I do my best to honor and respect them all, even the heavy and painful ones.

At the end of January, I began working a promotion that eventually led to me managing that promotion. I hired 3 of my friends to work with me (Badiyah, Jade and Larry) and we had fun while getting our work done. Jade came down from north Jersey almost every weekend to work with me. It was so nice to see her that often and be able to hang out with her and Badiyah together, for many of my friends have heard about each other, but haven't met. The two of them together were a TRIP!! Larry was the guy who was my manager (as well as Badiyah's) during the first promotion I ever worked. It was a pleasant and chill vibe. That lasted about 5 weeks before all hell broke loose.

That promotion company gave me a Scion (which was SPACIOUS inside, easy to park, never cost more than $30 to fill the tank and took about 8 hours to empty), company credit card, digital video camera, digital camera AND a Segway, while paying me $700/wk. The only problem was they weren't paying me quickly enough. My first day as a promotional model (some say "Brand

Ambassador") was January 29th. I didn't get paid anything, as a model or manager, until March 12th, give or take a day, and I'd been waiting every single day for it to arrive since the end of February when they first said that it was supposed to be at my place.

A check got lost in the mail, which I understand. What really upset me was that once they knew my check was lost, they slacked on issuing me another one while making repeated false promises (such as "I'll overnight it to you tomorrow") and made me look incompetent to my landlord (who is SO WONDERFUL). I did feel at risk of being evicted for I wondered how nice would he continue to be if these people didn't pay me? I told them all of this. My immediate boss didn't seem to care. The company that hired his company seemed to care more, but I'm not sure if they were sincere or not. My boss lied about so many things that I wasn't even surprised anymore.

I think that the experience was a karmic result of being involved with Eva. The lies and deception were all around me without me realizing it. The day I knew what she was about, I didn't even show up for a one-day promotion. I was getting paid cash at the end of the day and I could've used it too! When I think deeper about it, it was reflective of my own inner lies, for around this time I began to uncover what made me happiest. I dug in my pile of dirt until I reached a treasure beyond measure, which was music. In the beginning of February, I began to record me playing guitar and a few vocals using garage band and crappy headphones on my laptop. The musician within me was born.

Promotions that are in line with what I believe are the only ones I've been involving myself with lately to keep my spirit feeling harmonious. Every time I sign up to do one that isn't in line with my deeper beliefs, I end up changing my mind or not going at the last minute or quitting after a short period of time or something! Flaking out- on either end- bothers me. I'm doing my best to prevent that behavior from/to myself in arenas where showing up is important to whomever. I've found that I can push myself quite a distance- and happily- if I feel that the cause is worth the effort. I've gotten this far in life by pushing outwards in all directions from within, unfolding my petals with the power of my inner sunshine that's guided by the lights of the outer world.

Before my petals began to unfurl, I went through another great drama in February, helping out a friend from St. John named Sophie. Her sister came to Philly. Her name is Erika. Their mom is German and their dad is Iranian. Erika was staying with Sophie's mother-in-law in

Germantown, the neighborhood right next to mine. The woman
drove Erika crazy, so she asked to stay with me for one week and ended
up staying for 3 weeks because she found out that she was pregnant. It
was her husband's (they'd been married about 6 months), however, he
had just asked for a divorce. Erika had a return ticket back to St. John,
but she wasn't sure what to do now.

Erika decided to return to her homeland of Germany. Her baby's
father is black and white and lived on St. John, originally from Chicago
and Boston. We were curious as to how the baby would look and how to
go about custody and citizenship. Erika was very stressed out, for she
was only 23 years old. I did what I could to help. I was happy to have
the company car during that time to run her around to the clinic, get her
stuff, go to the airport, as well as the hospital. Twice we had to go to the
emergency room because she thought she had a miscarriage. The second
time, she was sure of it. She said that she saw the embryo.

It was an emotional time for me as well because she was the first
person I'd ever known whom I had been with through every step of the
pregnancy process- from the moment of finding out about being
pregnant until the moment of loss. It was very sad and a heavy burden
for her to bear alongside her husband's rejection (she wanted to stay
married regardless). She wanted the baby and accepted having it before
the first night that she started bleeding. She blamed herself the second
time for not staying off of her feet after going to the emergency room
that night, for 2 days later we were back again. This time Erika was
borderline hysterical, for she was positive that she lost the baby. I cried
for her loss as well.

The doctors kept her overnight drew blood and confirmed that
she had indeed lost the baby. No one did an internal exam. She didn't
want to go to another clinic. She was to leave for Germany in less than a
week. Health care was extremely cheap for good services there. She
received a bill from the Chestnut Hill Hospital prior to leaving that said
that she owed $6,000 for her 2 emergency room visits, where she waited
for about 10-12 hrs the first time and 12-14 hours the second time before
being seen by a doctor.

Come to find out, Erika is still pregnant!!! That is one strong
baby! After she thought she miscarried, she didn't go on a drinking or
drug spree (THANK GOODNESS!). She was more energetic doing all
kinds of things that she wouldn't have otherwise done. She would've
gone dancing if she could've. That's what she wanted to do. I had been
working and figuring out what was going on with my checks, I was so

broke and pmsing (emotional) that I wasn't up for going out. It was still pretty darn cold too!

Erika called me from Iran shortly after her return to Germany. She was visiting family. They wanted her to have an abortion because of the pending divorce and her age. Last I heard, she's living alone, near family, in a small city in Germany. She's expecting a healthy girl in the fall. The divorce is still pending. She intends to stay in Germany and go to school for nursing.

The baby's father and his brother used to be friends with me. They're the boys whom I stayed with during my last week on the island. I've talked to Erika's husband 2 or 3 times since I left. The last time was when they first got together. I spoke to her over the phone because Sophie had told me much about her. St. John's the one place I've lived where it's been difficult keeping in touch with the people from there, like Sophie, whom I called a few times throughout the year, but haven't heard from since I left.

Sophie and Erika were very appreciative of my help, for I treated Erika as I would've wanted to be treated had I been in her situation. It surprised me that some people, like Nina and Maxine, said that they wouldn't have done it. I'm not judging them negatively, I was simply surprised by their comments, for they are fairly nice women and attend Quaker meetings and it's a fundamental philosophy of that lifestyle to help people out. Quakers are big into outreach programs and being involved with the community. I've been to several meetings (their version of church) and have spoken (one is "moved" to speak or otherwise sit in silence). I love it. It is much harder to act on principles than it is to speak about them. I do understand and empathize with all those who take up mighty challenges every day in our world.

Erika's 3 week emotionally charged stay, combined with my terrible lifestyle habits (I was eating processed food, smoking, say 3- 4 cigarettes a day, drinking coffee, barely exercising, doing yoga or meditating and getting little sleep), our lack of money, the cluttered state of my apartment (I have a bunny and a cat too) and the loss of my sweet job during that time made the day of Erika's departure feel like heaven! I knew I'd miss her eventually. It wasn't anything personal against Erika. I was glad to have her as a close friend.

It rained in sheets the morning of our drive to the airport. As I began nearing home, it began to clear up. It was beautiful by that afternoon. I revel in my quiet time at home. It's a big reason I choose to live alone, so that I have ample quiet time at my disposal. Erika was home pretty much all the time those three weeks and she's not as clean as I am. She wasn't a slob, simply not as clean or neat as I am. She made efforts, which I did appreciate.

There was more stuff around in general, on top of her buying shit, especially food that was unnecessary and somewhat expensive when I had no money. It was hard to see the waste. I did my best to be available emotionally to her during my own emotionally turbulent times. It was the worst time to have premenstrual syndrome. The week before Erika left, I cried almost every day from stress. The weekend of Erika's departure was a pivotal moment in my life.

When I heard "Please don't go" by The Roots, it was the Friday night before Erika left on Sunday. As the song played I was overcome with a deep happiness and feelings of love, bliss and pain from within that made me want to sing, dance and scream all at the same time. I wasn't familiar with The Roots' music prior to, so I'm not even sure what made me click on Black Thought's profile on myspace. It's a "demo" song. It wasn't on any of their cds. This song found me and in my deepest despair, music once again saved me.

I was at Nina's house to do laundry and escape my own place. I played that song over and over again on her computer (she was an awesome friend that night. I had her place all to myself for hours) and enjoyed the loud vibrations while I could, for my laptop speakers only go so loud and the song wasn't available to download or purchase. It anchored me in the midst of my chaotic storm. That song allowed me to feel my frustrations in ways that expressed a sweet, melodic, sensual pain.

I had heard how amazing The Roots' live shows are and that they've been around forever. I knew that they were a top notch group from Philly. My friends in high school were heavily into rap and hip-hop, so their name has been around me since '93. I only knew one song of theirs though- or so I thought. Months later, after getting their cds, I realized that I know a BUNCH of their songs and that many are hip-hop classics. They brought back many memories hearing them as part of the soundtrack to my life.

While in Seattle, I learned "The Seed" because Derek, Bill and Ariana loved playing it in the garage and at shows. I rapped Black Thought's verses. Ariana would sometimes rap with me. Me and another woman sang Cody Chestnut's parts (the chorus). I think there's a tape somewhere from one of the shows where we performed that song. We did a pretty decent job, especially considering I had never rapped before and we didn't perform hip-hop or rap music. For real though, I had no idea whose shoes I was filling. I soon learned.

I don't have a professional artist's lifestyle quite yet, but I am still happy most of the time and I love and am loved every second of the day. That is enough for me. I am used to dealing with "far-fetched" ideas and making them my reality, like living in paradise. The experience of my ideas in reality are even more amazing than the vision or dream- that is important to remember. They are very much worth any and all struggles, for EACH of US are worth the effort.

That Friday night, in mid March, while listening to "Please Don't Go", I wrote to Black Thought via myspace asking him if there was any way I could download the song so that I could hear it properly (loudly, on my stereo) any time I wanted. The next day he sent me a message via myspace asking me how I was doing. I told him the truth about my stressed out life. In the next message, he gave me his cell phone number. I thought I was being punk'd (like the MTV show) in some way. I told Erika about it. She LOVES hip-hop and wanted me to call him right away. I was too much of an emotional wreck. I wanted some down time first before contacting anyone new- famous or not.

I called the number Sunday afternoon. I had looked up Black Thought's real name, Tariq Trotter, to see if this guy knew it. He did, but for whatever reason, I wasn't fully convinced. I didn't mention that I was unsure if it was really him. The profile looked legit, but the circumstances seemed too strange, even for me, yet my life IS a bit odd, so I went with it. He invited me to their studio to hear The Roots' new album- "Game Theory"- due to be released in several months. Was this guy for real??

On Tuesday, I had to return the promo car to Princeton, NJ and pick up my check from some of the worst employers I've ever had the misfortune of having, so I decided to go check it out the next night, Monday, AFTER asking Larry (who worked with King Britt and was familiar with Philly's hip-hop places) if The Roots had a studio at the same location this guy told me. It was exact, to the floor number, so I was fairly certain I wasn't being punk'd, but only 60 percent sure. It could've been a practical joke or something. People are crazy in Philadelphia! I wasn't going to believe it until I saw him AND the studio.

People can be mean as well. I've experienced this enough in my lifetime. I had no idea if The Roots got their kicks out of contacting girls on myspace and making them meet them at a certain location to film them walking around in circles hoping and expecting to see their "favorite artist". My momma didn't raise no fool!! or did she?? (and I'm an "optimist"!) It took a minute for me to get a hold of Tariq on the phone once I arrived. I almost left. I couldn't find the right set of stairs. I didn't really know what he looked like because I never paid attention to him before and photos can look totally different. He was very helpful though, once I did reach him. I felt at ease almost immediately. Yup, this guy was most definitely for real.

The place was huge, with many rooms. I sat in a living room type of area at first, shooting the shit with the guys who were around. I had not one clue whether any of them were famous or not. I only knew of Questlove (the hair) and knew that he wasn't there. I felt like I should've known more about the group, but then I thought that it might be better that I didn't know. I didn't want to offend anyone by NOT recognizing him or her though. I soon discovered that for the most part, the people I met were all mature men who simply cared about good music (and good food), not who recognized them. We all talked about things that I talk about with many other guys who put their intelligence to positive use. They were nice, cool and much healthier than what I expected.

It took a couple of hours before the studio was available for our listening purposes. Engineers were in there along with a couple of other people that had something to do with the new music that was about to inundate my being. When I first began listening, it was hard to control my enthusiasm. The urge to dance was so strong. I moved around on the sofa doing my best not to cause a commotion or look like a freak.

During the first couple of songs I was so impressed and moved to say some things to Tariq that I rambled on a bit. He valued my feedback and loved that I was digging the music, but I missed some things (like his amazing lyrics) by talking. He calmly suggested that I simply be quiet until the cd was over. I realized, "Oh shit!! I'm in The Roots' studio listening to their new album!" and I didn't want the music to end. I hadn't thought about being able to replay it soon. When I found out that the cd wasn't being released until the END of August, I was disappointed, but grateful to have had a taste. I told them all that I'd be very proud in their shoes. Shortly afterwards, Tariq walked me to the door. I gave him a hug, thanked him for the entire experience and left.

'Twas Bono, of U2, who popped my "celebrity cherry" though and made me feel just as special as he is when I was fifteen years old. I was in Hershey, Pa with my brother during his Homecoming. U2 stopped in Hershey during that time en route to Philly for a show, I

believe. Friends of my brother invited me to go with them to the
hotel they stayed at the previous two days. They were seen outside
talking to people and signing autographs. I liked some songs from
"Joshua Tree" and liked a couple off of "Achtung Baby", which had just
come out. It was the Zoo TV tour.

The night before, I wrote a letter to Bono that said that I'd love
to get to know him and included my phone number. I truly just wanted
to hang out with him and thought that it was so "far-fetched" that it just
might happen! When we arrived at the hotel, the crowd had grown to a
size that was not conducive to anything casual. I stood by the sidelines
hoping just to see him in person.

Bono came out the front door with the rest of the band. They said
that they had to get to rehearsal and wouldn't be able to sign autographs.
That's when Bono came up to me (I've truly no idea why), put his arm
around me and asked me how I was doing. I didn't think I'd be
speechless, but I was. It was like a time warp. I knew that my time was
limited, so it all felt like slow motion. I told him that I was fine and
asked how he was (walking with his arm around me, mind you). I had a
sharpee and no paper, so I asked him to sign his san pellogrino (mineral
water) bottle for me. He smiled and did it. I remembered my letter and
slipped it in his pocket. We hugged goodbye and that was that.

The boys drove off in their white, convertible Cadillac and I went
off with my brothers friends, whom I left when Bono whisked me away!
The most fantastic thing was blasting Achtung Baby on the highway and
looking over and seeing them driving along in that big-ass Cadillac! I
didn't have a camera. I don't even know if the girls took pictures. I'm
not much for "keepsakes". My mom has kept the signed bottle half my
life now. It's more her bottle than it is mine and it bothers me none.

At the end of March '06, Lauryn Hill-Marley started a profile on
myspace. I was one of the first to see it. I knew that it was new because
she had so few friends still. I knew it was really her because Questlove
had just added her to his top 8. So I decided to write to her thinking that
she just might write me back- and she did.

Her reply (I was going to include it, but I can't reach her again to
ask her permission and it was personal), along with the first song that
she uploaded to her profile ("Foxy") before it was even a "music
profile", made me feel like I was on top of the world! Ms. Hill-Marley is
a very different woman from me, but I see her as a kindred spirit. The
fact that she was humble enough to write to me, that we connected at all,
solidified this feeling. It meant a lot to me as did the fact that she was

genuine and real as a human being. It was awesome and inspiring for me, as a person, woman and artist. It's how I envision myself being-regardless of "status", which can be a huge challenge for many people involved in the entertainment industry.

It is not "just a coincidence" that I heard and fell in love with "The Miseducation of Lauryn Hill" while in St. John or that I hadn't heard much of The Roots' material (but had covered a song of theirs) prior to this year. The aforementioned as well as Eve, Will Smith and Jill Scott are all from the Philly, NY, & DC area and are people who have indirectly and directly helped to shape me as a person, woman and artist. Lauryn, Wyclef and I have that Caribbean love also which, once experienced, is always present. For me, there is no going back in my heart. The islands are a part of me forever.

One day, Ms. Hill-Marley removed "Foxy"- after a week or so. I was listening to it a few times a day. I was so sad because I LOVED that song. It made me get up to sing and dance almost every time I heard it. I felt on top of the world when it played. Within a week (nothing was up in the interim), she had 10 songs up on her profile, which had now officially become a music profile, most of which were available for download. I could hardly believe it!!!

ANOTHER "UNLIKELY" DREAM HAD COME TRUE!!! For I checked back almost every day to see if "Foxy" was back up, letting out deep sighs every time I saw that it wasn't there. I downloaded all of her new songs and immediately BLASTED them in my stereo DELIGHTED from head to toe! My soul soared!! I was especially happy when shortly thereafter, only a few songs remained. Finally, only one song was left up there. None have been available to download since that time. Only one is there right now. "Foxy" is my miracle song.

Luck?? I rarely use the word. Consciousness is more like it. As I mentioned earlier, like energies attract other like energies, which makes me think of a musician named Tony Saks. Once I moved to Mt. Airy, I sought out this guy that I heard play guitar years ago (Nina loved his music when we were friends the first time), the one who I thought might attract Maxine to a show, for they attended high school together. I knew he was very talented at singing, songwriting and playing the guitar. I wanted to see how much he charged for guitar lessons and I hoped that he would feel my songs enough to collaborate with me on them.

I asked around the neighborhood seeing if anyone knew this guy. I knew he was a dedicated musician and was still out there, but no one I came across knew him. Lotus thought the name sounded familiar and suggested that I look under her friends list on myspace, for she thought she worked with him a few years prior, but wasn't sure if it was the same guy. I couldn't remember what Tony looked like, but I came across a profile under her friends that I thought sounded like him. A couple of weeks go by and I hear back from him. BINGO! I'd found him!!

Tony was really nice. He gave me his phone number. He lived within walking distance of me, so we made tentative plans (this was in October, when I actually had some free/down time and was with Ty) and got together twice within a couple of weeks. He gave me a cd of his music each time I saw him. I'd never heard so much of his music before, just three or four songs years ago.

Being with Ty at the time made me uncomfortable in ways because I was so in love with Tony's music. His music alone made me feel emotions that made my relationship with Ty crystal clear- that we were not in love the way I enjoy being romantically. It was hard for me to separate the man from the music. It messed with me for a few months, especially after Ty and I broke up. I was communicative with Tony as to my feelings all along the way, perhaps too much. He's a male Sagittarius, they tend not to like that.

The month of November was pretty much ALL about the movie- and sleep. I started teaching myself guitar (on an acoustic that Lotus left) in October, but only picked it up here and there in November. I love playing the guitar. I used to "play" rubber bands when I was kid- like B.B. King. I love the sounds of string instruments. They manipulate my emotions in ways that bring about some of the most profound musical experiences I've ever known, which was ONE of the reasons I was so drawn to Tony.

I was pleasantly surprised to be so moved by Tony's music. I told him in an email (we hung out with each other once, after my break up with Ty) sometime around mid-December that I am attracted to him, but that I don't care to pursue anything sexual with him- or anyone- for at least another 5-6 months. I felt I had had enough sexual experiences for a while.

Tony didn't seem to have a problem with this, but I haven't hung out with him since then. I've been to a nearby café to watch him perform anywhere from 15 min to 2 hours (rarely was I ever there when he began his set). He performs there every Friday. I made it there when I thought of it, felt like it and was available. I enjoy his music and have often said that I would rather see musicians I love in smaller venues, before they're famous. It seemed like I made Tony a little uncomfortable at times though, so I went only when I felt like his reaction to me wouldn't matter whatsoever. I was all about the music, which fascinated and entranced me.

I often sang his songs around the house. His songs about love and life filled me with reverie and hope. When I first began listening to Tony's music, I felt connected to life in ways that I hadn't in way too long. His music is what made me begin to realize that what I had with Ty was not the kind of romance that I envisioned having for myself/life. Tony was gloriously singing about that kind of romance. I knew that's what I lived for, but not necessarily to be shared with him. It was so easy to associate those feelings with Tony though, seeing as he expressed them so well, however, I did not really know him and he wasn't giving me much opportunity.

Eva was a very good diversion for a while. I told her all about Tony. Nina knew Tony through Maxine. Nina and Maxine both knew how I felt about Tony. It was a very common occurrence for women to fall in love with Tony. He was sincere, nice, relatively humble and so full of talent, singing about love and life in funny and touching ways with a voice of a rock n' roll possessed angel and the passion to match. Nina was in love with a guitarist as well and fanned my flames alongside her own.

Larry had given me his digital camera to log the footage I'd taken on our road trip for work, with him and Badiyah. Remember the video camera I mentioned having for work? I put it to personal use. I love filming! What can I say? I had his camera for about 2 weeks before he left for a year long promotional tour, so I taped a show of Tony's. It was the first time I'd seen him perform with a drummer and bassist. The bassist used to go to high school with me. I worked for his brother this past winter doing promotions (small world). The show was terrific! I got there between sets. Batteries were charged and I was ready to go! I got the entire second half of the show.

I took photographs as I taped the show. I was excited to see how it all came out and to share it with the guys. As soon as I got home, I began the process of uploading everything, editing the photos and video footage, transferring, sending, etc. I attempted to email Tony the video footage, but it wouldn't go through. To avoid further problems, I used my mac account to host a webpage for him so that whomever he wanted to see his show and/or photos could easily view them.

Quicktime is a software used to watch the videos on the website I built. Tony was still having trouble watching them, so I figured out a way to transfer the videos to my desktop and upload them to myspace, where he could easily get the html codes and post them wherever he felt like on there. Mind you, I had 11 songs of his that EACH took time to compress, upload, transfer and send, along with the 80 or so photos I'd taken. This "spur of the moment" project took me the better part of 3 days to complete. I happily did it out of support for his music and to gain the experience in a field that is a passion of mine.

Tony was very appreciative. I'd been asking him to hang out since January, but he never made time for me and he didn't still. I wondered when we'd ever hang out again. The time was drawing near. I wasn't alluding to anything romantic either. I truly just wanted to spend some time with the guy, seeing as I think he's an artistic genius. A week after I taped the show, Nina and I (first time she'd ever come with me) went to see Tony perform solo. We had a good time listening to him and talking amongst ourselves about the feelings he (his music) stirs in me, among other things.

Nina invited Tony out to eat with us. He wanted to finish a musical (That's Tony. He pretty much wrote the whole thing in a weekend.) before going out that night, but he was up for meeting us for drinks or something later. I was greatly disappointed that I had to work. I considered calling out. He said that we could do something later in the week. I was happy to see that he was finally opening up to me and sincerely wanted to hang out that week.

I started adhering to a strictly vegan and primarily organic diet in the beginning of April. I also began biking, doing yoga, meditating, walking and work out tapes on a regular basis. By the time I saw Tony (about a month later, at the show I taped), the weather had gotten warmer (less clothing) and my body was becoming well defined. I drank lots more water too. It all caused my energy level to increase in ways I'd forgotten about. All of this, I believed, played a factor in Tony being interested in spending a little time with me now. Then I went and did it. I took my enthusiasm too far, without a clue that I was doing something that could be construed as harmful.

Shortly after I'd heard Tony's music in the fall, I mentioned the idea of putting together a compilation cd of my favorite tracks of his, writing a review of all the songs and submitting it to a local radio station that has an audience who'd love his music. The idea had been in my head since then. He hadn't voiced any concerns about it when I brought it up then, so when the idea returned to me full force the same weekend that he agreed to hang out, I thought, "How lovely it'd be if he heard a song of his playing on the radio."

I wrote out a professional, yet personal, email to the staff at WXPN declaring my love of Tony Saks' music - as a fan. I told them that I'd hung out with him a few times, but that we're not friends. I sent his music via email to give them the opportunity to listen to his material. I've no idea what transpired on their end, but on this end, I thought I'd done something to further my friend's musical career and help share his music with so many others whom I felt would love his music just as much as I do. I sent him a copy of the email so that he could read what I had written.

The very next day, Tony called and left a message on my voicemail saying that he needed to talk to me. I wanted to believe that it was for a good reason, but I could tell that he was not happy. The only thing that I thought he might be upset with that I wrote was that "he's not your 'typical' good-looking guy, but he is attractive". Tony didn't mention that part. The fact that I said that he's humble, sincere and 29 were the things that he vocalized complaints about in reference to the email I sent.

He is recording an album soon and has a plan for his work that he didn't want me to ruin. I had no idea. If he'd taken the time to talk to me during the times I'd made available (even via email) for us to discuss our work (which I mentioned), I would've had some clue as to where Tony saw his music heading and possibly wouldn't have caused him such headaches and grief. The way he reacted made it seem like I'd done irrevocable damage to his career, which I don't think is the case. I didn't say anything that bad. Irrevocable damage to our friendship is another story.

I apologized profusely to Tony pleading ignorance and naivety. He knew me well enough to realize there was no malicious intent on my part and that I aimed to help. That didn't matter to him. I asked him to call me later on in the week. I sent an apologetic email later on that day. I have not heard from him since. I began to wonder, "Perhaps many of the feelings he shares in his music are memories from times past. He might not be that same person- so full of life and love." For I strongly feel that part of loving people is forgiving them, for just about all of us on earth make mistakes at one point or another. Few of us recognize our mistakes and wholeheartedly ask forgiveness for them. If my friend isn't willing to value this and move on, then they aren't the kind of friend I care to have close to me.

Deep down, I think that Tony is loving and will forgive me one day, but right now, he's probably mired in all the bullshit that comes with making a living as a full-time artist in our modern world/times. Perhaps in the future, he'll take a more compassionate tone with me- and others like me. I still listen to his music and feel good singing it, but it isn't the same. I don't have the same reverence towards it. It is sometimes difficult to separate the man from the music (I wrote a long blog about this topic). Music tells its own story though and all we have to do is listen.

Chapter 6
WHO/WHAT/WHERE/WHY/HOW I AM NOW

My nickname is Blue. I forgot to mention up until now that within two weeks upon my arrival to St. John, a Rastafarian local, whom I never saw again, asked me for my name. I said, "Kristyn". He said, "Nah. Give me another name." The first thing that came out was, "Blue" and he said, "Yeah, yeah, I like that.", as did I, very much. Blue is all over the Caribbean in just about every shade of the color. I absolutely love it. It reminds me of beautiful waters, clear skies, tranquility, music, deep emotions, sunrises (especially dawn) and sunsets (especially twilight). I love that it's only 4 letters and I spell it just like the color. Many people misspell Kristyn, even close friends and family who mean no harm, and oftentimes confuse it with many of its variances: Christina, Kirsten, Crystal, Krista, Christine, etc. I love the name Kristyn as well as Lynette and Simmons. Each of my 3 names have 7 letters. They all add up to 21. Those 3 numbers are the ones that I feel resonate most with me.

Many people label me many things. I accept them all, for my essence is (what I call) love, which is every thing and no thing. What I'm doing with this awareness is living my life in ways that help me to remember this fact as much and as often as possible and do my best to allow others to feel this love we are and I speak of, if and as they so choose in ways that create win/win situations all around. I am using all sorts of mediums to share what I've learned, how I've learned it and what I envision on earth, which is similar to Dr. Martin Luther King's visions in his "I have a dream" speech.

Hearing that speech still brings tears to my eyes oftentimes when I hear it. Each time, I recall reciting it with my classmates in second grade, being exposed to it for the first time and believing in his words whole heartedly, for I knew that I was a product of his vision that not many people, not so long ago, in America, believed. THANK YOU SO MUCH- to all of those who did believe, who continue to believe, and who expand upon his ideas, even though not all have come to fruition-yet. Patience is, in deed, a virtue. It is this faith and determination in things unseen that moves me from one "failure" to the next "joy" and the next "pain", for they all go hand-in-hand in building strong foundations for great things to exist. For what doesn't kill us DOES make us stronger in some way.

Traveling is one of my favorite things to do. Exploring different cultures offers me perspective, among other things. I see what changes and what stays the same, in relation to me, and others, in all sorts of ways. Living in Philadelphia this time around is the longest I've been in one place, consecutively, since I first left when I was 19 years old. It's hilarious to me that I'm so in love with Philly for the first time 10 years after leaving. Somehow it seems fitting, like the story of "The Prodigal Son", which I know of from the church I grew up in, Emanuel Lutheran Church at 4th and Washington Sts., which is right next to where my grandmother and eldest aunt now live- a half block from where I used to live as a kid. I could easily see the church and high rise building next to it from the roof of my apartment near 4th and South Sts.

I plan to have a home in Philly someday (my mom and Nana might live in it), as well as other places. I don't care to live an extravagant lifestyle. I'm not sure quite yet where I'll be, when I'll be there or for how long. Everyone in my life knows this truth. It's one of the reasons I like the whole "BE HERE NOW" (Ram Dass) philosophy. It's a challenge to live by in this day and age, but those simple words have helped me tremendously (the book is excellent!) throughout the years.

The countries I'd most like to visit are: India, Brazil, Italy, France, Ireland, Ghana, Egypt, Mali, the Ivory Coast, Greece, Finland, New Zealand, Australia, Fiji, Indonesia, Nepal, Japan, Thailand, Holland, Belize and Costa Rica. There are others, of course, those are simply at the top of my immediate list which doesn't include all of the places where my friends are whom I'm so looking forward to seeing again!

Joseph Campbell was a world-renowned mythologist who wrote many books on the topic of mythology and its vital role in cultures all around the world. I've watched his "Power of Myth" series, an interview with Bill Moyers that aired on PBS, a few times by borrowing it from the library. It's a 6 part series (there's a written record published in book form as well) that made me wish to know what that man knew. He died in 1987 at 83 years old having happily done what he urged many others to do, which was simply, "Follow your bliss." Seems so simple, but as Bruce Lee once said in an on camera interview, "I can show you many fancy tricks and impress you with my moves, but to express oneself honestly, now THAT, my friend, is very hard to do."

We've lost so many leaders in our country that stood for civil freedoms, spiritual values and moral principles that were in line with

harmonious ways of living for all human beings on this earth. I look
to extend those harmonious ways to all life on earth. The lives of people
like: Malcolm X, Ida B. Wells, Dr. Martin Luther King Jr., Sojourner
Truth, Thich Nhat Hahn, W.E.B. DuBois, Angela Davis, John Lennon,
The Dalai Lama, Robert Kennedy, Ghandi and Bruce Lee were not lived
in vain and my current plan is in action to showcase this truth. All of
those people- and so many more- are whom I call upon for strength,
guidance, love and support.

They are a handful of the lives that have inspired and touched
me- and the world- with their quality of life and perseverance in the
midst of great struggle. Some of those lives ceased to be in human form
due to the violence of which they were opposed. It's appeared to me
that's it's made many afraid to stand up for things that the "Flower
Power" generation were known for advocating representing.

I am a flower that arose through a crack in the sidewalk of a
concrete jungle and I'm quite sure I'm not the only one. My friends and
others out there reminding me that no, I am not alone and our numbers
are growing. In this case, I truly do feel like, "The more the merrier!!",
which has rarely been the case for me. I've oftentimes preferred intimate
gatherings, but these days, I am embracing multitudes more and more.

I do what I do because I love it. I've relaxed enough within
mySelf/Life/Love to know what my bliss is and trust it enough to follow
it, using the faculties of my heart, intuition, emotions, mind and body, in
that order too. It's a ride, that's for sure! Being primarily asexual (single,
by choice, happily, indefinitely) and a woman in my thirties keeps me on
my toes in all areas, especially emotionally. The most challenging thing
I find is that not many others are used to relating to life in ways that I do.
This makes me more susceptible to losing my focus and doing things
that aren't in line with all of me, which can cause a degree of imbalance
in my life. I get what I put in. I see on the outside what I'm creating
from the inside of me. As long as I pay attention along the way, I can
clearly see what is happening.

Yoga helps me stay calm while moving my body. Some people
think that yoga is just stretching. Those are the people that tend to take a
class and find out that stretching is a PART of yoga, but that there's
much more to it, including, but not limited to, a good muscular work
out, depending on the form. Yoga literally means "union". I've read
before that the word "sin" means to see yourself as separate. To
elaborate: "to 'sin' is to see yourself as being separate from God." I
grew up Lutheran and see the potential to see this is as blasphemous,

however, if one said to his parent, "Am I part of you?" Whichever parent would most likely say, "Of course!! Your father/mother and I created you."

That's the idea, I believe, to remember that we are whole or one with God/The Creator. That there are no real divisions, but the ones WE CREATE in our societies for the sake of ease in communication and understanding, but we oftentimes get caught up in the labels and forget to see without "sin", to "become one". Yoga centers me in the midst of movement and stillness. It makes me take note of my breath, which is truly what keeps me alive in this form. Yoga causes me to stop and honor my breath by simply being with it, like one cares to just be with that "whatever/whomever", when you're feeling all in love. Time stands still and you relish it. You allow yourself to be/feel "one" with "everything".

On Monday, May 15th, my client dropped me off at home after training and I didn't leave my property until that Saturday, May 20th, in the afternoon. From Monday- Thursday, I birthed 4 musical children using garage band, the built-in microphone on my laptop and a pair of ratty headphones. I could hardly believe what had come out of me. It seemed like I was channeling pure spirit because it was so easy for me to do all that I was doing even though I had never used the loops I came across on garage band. I hardly ever used garage band before!!

Back in February, I recorded 4 songs- all instrumental. One song came unexpectedly during that recording session. It's called, "Om". I liked all of the songs more than I thought I would. I planned on making a song once a week, but I got too caught up with Erika and the drama with work and life (way off "center" then). I recorded the guitar jams mainly to see how easy or hard it was to create a music profile on myspace. It was pretty darn easy! Many of my friends liked what took less than an hour to record. I liked it too, but knew I could do more and better.

This time on garage band, I meant business! I had recorded 3 songs (2 originals) and 5 songs (3 originals) other times and had lost both cds over the course of moving. Mike, who stored the masters, didn't have them anymore, so I had nothing. I was tired of not having any of my music (with lyrics) recorded. Working on my songs and hearing how they came out made me feel like a female version of Pharell. I know he's much better than me, but I see remarkable potential given the right equipment.

The same could be said for many people of all ages who have talent, yet no money to buy the right equipment to bring out their latent abilities. I encourage every person to do just as Joseph Campbell said and "Follow your bliss." I think of it as a feeling inside that is a natural high of supreme happiness, like a spiritual, emotional and mental orgasm. As long as we keep stimulating ourselves, we will eventually climax. Rest is equally as important as stimulation and intense experiences. Life is cyclical like that, but there are peaks and valleys along the way, for that's movement/foreplay. We have to build momentum to orgasm and thus a dream (idea) is born into the world. It's crucial not to get stuck on things though and to know that these feelings are not ones that can be bought, sold or traded, but are produced from deep within one's psyche.

One of the ways I look to "give back to my community" is to start a program that makes instruments and equipment cheap, free and/or available to those in lower economic neighborhoods who look to use them to further themselves in some way (artistically, professionally, therapeutically or otherwise). For Philadelphia in particular, I'd really like to see better education in public schools, better pay for teachers, more community centers and outreach programs in poorer neighborhoods and things to build principles and pride in people tangibly and consistently.

Sometimes in order to see if we enjoy something or if it's a good fit, we have to go on and experience it. There are ways to prepare for the experience, but no thing is the experience of the thing. Close enough at times can be good enough. But if something, like making music, is your passion, (as I have just fully realized recently), there is no going back until what is seen behind the eyes is seen in front of them.

Music comes from a place within me that makes me feel Divine. It is MY bliss- one I now openly share with others. In ways, "others" made me not want to see myself in the public eye, for I didn't want my music and my life to be publicly scrutinized. This was when I didn't even know I wanted to be a musician. Then I wasn't even sure what kind of music I'd write. Fame was a risk that I wasn't willing to take in being a musician. I could hide behind books. It's only now that I feel truly comfortable baring my soul to the world in a way that I've held sacred and have admired in other people my entire life.

I have 7 songs now. There are many more in my head and heart that I've yet to get out. After I finished my first batch of songs and uploaded them onto myspace (that was an exercise in patience due to technical difficulties on their end), I started to have this overwhelming urge to finish this book, even though I wanted to make more music. The period of "technical difficulties" gave me time to fine-tune my songs as best I could on my own (without professional equipment or engineers). I look forward to getting back to playing guitar and recording.

It's ALL a bunch of cycles~

my Love, Life.

Chapter 7
My Commitment to Love/Life

Monday, May 22, 2006 (a week ago) was my 7-year anniversary- the day I married Nature, my Self and Raphael.

These are the vows that I read aloud that day. I wrote them a few days before we got married:

WEDDING VOWS
Saturday, May 22, 1999

I, Kristyn Lynette Simmons, vow to honor, respect and be loyal to Raphael. I will learn compassion with him and grow with him through happy and sad times. I have been, am, and will continue to be honest with him in thought, word and deed. I dedicate my life towards the expression of his true self and I promise to love him and appreciate him for who he was in the past, who he is in the present and for whom he will be in our future.

Lately, I've been noticing numerous patterns and things that are connected in ways that are way beyond my ego's planning skills. I WEPT repeatedly during the week I created my songs because of the energy that flowed through me so heavily and powerfully. It felt incredible. It still does. I'm just not crying as often- I had PMS then too....every 28-30 days... I've heard some say that 29 is a major year. It's been 7 years since I've been this in love, happy and at peace with life and even then, I knew that it wasn't because of Raphael. He came along at a very good time and enhanced all that I was already feeling for I could easily relate to him on that level, which I found so strange then, but don't think so now.

I am single and have been for over 6 months. I have a cat that is my sunshine and a bunny that I've grown to appreciate. I'm completely financially poor, some times making ends meet, yet I feel beside myself with glee on a daily basis these days, for all things change, not just some of them, which has been one of my hardest lessons in life. As Juliet says, "And this too, shall pass." It applies to the "good" and "bad" in life.

One of my favorite lines, from The Little Prince, "'What is essential is invisible to the eye.' The little prince repeated so that he would be sure to remember.", reminds of this fundamental thing~ our essence. "Me", "You", "Us" have nothing to do with money, power, fame or beauty. It can't be counted or measured, but you'll know it when you find it, if you haven't already. If you haven't found it, seek it! It IS essential.

The Greeks knew what they were talking about when they coined the old adage, "Know thyself", for knowledge is, in DEED/ACTION power. Some people find themselves drawn to me and aren't sure why. For many, I think it's their inner-self seeing itself. It yearns to express itself. Some feel exuberant around me and we get high off of each other's energy, while some others are infuriated by me for I reflect the anger and frustration they feel within themselves. I've had all kinds of reactions to my energy over the years. For the most part, I tend to meet other kindred spirits and have serendipitous experiences regularly.

Speaking of which, last summer, I was on my way to a promotional training when I heard someone say, "Kristyn??" I thought it was someone from high school because I'm so used to hearing "Blue" now. I'm not always happy to see someone from my high school, so I slowly turned around and saw that it was Nathan!! I had JUST emailed his brother's band mates to see if they had any way of reaching Nathan or his brother (who was no longer in the band). I had come across some photos of Nathan and wondered how he was doing.

Lo and behold, he was standing in front of me 2 days later, with a patch over his eye. Philadelphia has one of the best eye clinics in the country. Nathan had come to Philly, and had been staying with his sister, who lives right outside of Philly, all week because he had to have eye surgery. His right eye had to be removed. He had cancer of the eye. I don't think it was due to heroin use, but I'm not sure. I didn't ask him about his use. It had been 3 years since I'd seen him. I had a feeling that he was still using or else I think he would've said something or at the very least, he would've kept in touch. We exchanged numbers and emails. I called him a couple of times, but then he vanished into thin air again.

I contacted Luke after a year of no contact since I was feeling better and cared not to harbor any negative feelings towards anyone in the world. I had come across several things within a short period of time that reminded me of him. I figured that he was still with the ex-girlfriend that showed back up on the island. I felt much better and looked to make any "troubled" relationships "untroubled", if I could. Facing my feelings towards Luke was a big deal, bigger than I first realized. Many of the pleasurable feelings I'd been starting to feel reminded me of the last time I'd felt that happy, which was in St. John, before Luke ended things between us, which was a very painful time. It was tough revisiting those feelings at first, but I'm glad that I did.

I called Luke a few times over the course of 3 weeks (in April). He didn't return any of my calls. I got his girlfriend once. I hoped that my calls weren't causing any friction. Come to find out, Luke had broken up with his girlfriend. She had his phone that day and didn't tell him that I called. He had lost my phone number and had problems figuring out how to call me from the voicemails I left (that phone was gone, he just checked the messages) until finally he succeeded in leaving me a voicemail.

Luke's voicemail message came as a pleasant surprise. He sounded happy to hear from me. He said that he had called a bunch of times, but I hadn't received any messages (he was hanging up before sending them through the system, which deleted them). It felt weird to be so happy to talk to him. I felt a sense of betrayal from myself since we'd gone a whole year without contact due to his loyalty to his girlfriend whom he always thought of as being a "bad girlfriend". The year before, this offended me for I put up with way too much of his shit to go days without a return phone call when I expressed urgency in talking to him, as a friend. He was a crappy friend during that time and it pissed me off.

Forgiveness is fantastic, in it's true form, as is compassion. Luke was hurt by my decision to leave St. John for he thought that it meant that I wasn't really in love with him. He did the best he could with what he knew and had to work with from within. I love him and genuinely care about his well-being. I acknowledged what happened and made my feelings clear- to clarify for him and I wanted to hear from him that he'd choose a better way in the future. No verbal "lashings" were given. The time we spent apart was painful enough, for we enjoy each other's presence in one another's lives.

We are in frequent contact now. In fact, Luke won his first boat race ever this past weekend and I was one of the first people he called to share the news. I was so happy for him and glad to hear the sound of shock and pride in his voice at his victory. That's one of the best parts about having real friends- sharing in miserable AND joyous occasions, for neither are as fun for long by yourself.

Jean painted 12 outstanding oil paintings after we broke up. He's much more healthy. He quit smoking for a while and doesn't drink nearly as much as he used to, which all makes him enjoy his life more. He went through periods where he didn't date anyone in order to focus on his work. We spoke of this while we were together, for I found that throughout my life, I've done so much more while single as opposed to when I'm romantically entwined with someone. Producing major work is a huge reason I choose to be asexual for a while.

Life expresses itself in all sorts of ways. Jean painted one painting while we were together, even though I had an art studio for 2 of the 5 months we were dating. I'd love to have a collection of his work in my home. It's visceral and thought provoking, with well balanced, vibrant oil colors and imaginative designs. He asked me to sit for one of them in the next couple of days. This will be my first time modeling for him- other than 1 or 2 drawings he did while we were dating. I'm just so pleased at how far we've come as friends, considering a year ago, I didn't think it was probable for Jean to be a good, platonic friend to me any time soon.

Raphael is touring Asia right now on behalf of his art, which is modern and innovative. He just had a showing in Rockefeller center for 2 weeks (an exhibit of international artists). I did my best to get up there to see him for a couple of hours, but it didn't work out. His cell phone wasn't working. I wasn't sure which day was best. After not seeing him in 5 years, I preferred to spend some serious time with him and chill for a bit anyway. I told him that I will do what I can to visit him once he returns to the States in August. I still sense that Raphael doesn't fully trust me, but he trusts me a WHOLE lot more than he did during the first half of our years together. I'm impressed with how far he has come and am grateful and proud to call him a close friend.

I've had a tarot deck since I was 17 or 18 years old, a deck based on Greek mythology. Before this year, I hadn't touched them in 5-7 years. Nina just discovered the tarot and reawakened my interest. The Mayan Calendar is another "alternative practice" that I used to follow years ago (for months before I met Raphael and for about a year afterwards) that I've brought back into my life. I've been thinking of books that I've read that I would like to revisit as well as others I've heard about, like "The Four Agreements", by don Miguel Ruiz. I ended up buying, reading and giving mom "The Four Agreements". We both enjoyed it and found it very useful.

My relationship with my mom and my brother is sustained because of our faith in the invisible. We are all water signs; our emotions run deep. I am proud of my family- all of them. They've been there for me in mind, body and spirit not just through my ups and my downs, but their own as well. Seeing the people at Emanuel Lutheran Church is like seeing extended family members for many have known me since I was a kid and love me as if I was that same child. I love them so very much as well.

Kyah (the one who protected me as a kid, my favorite cousin) lives 10 minutes away from me now, as does my mom, brother, the kids and 2 of my aunts and cousins. It's the best!! I'd love to buy a house in Mt. Airy and move more of my family here. I know that some will not leave south Philly, which is fine. I see them the least, but I'm always so happy when I do. We'll have to make more efforts to bridge that gap. With efforts, results will show.

My mom used to be the only one, other than one uncle, who lived anywhere outside of south Philly. It's wonderful to be so much closer to my family, in every which way, even though I know many will have smart things to say about all that I've mentioned- and didn't mention. I learned very young that I will be quite unhappy living my life trying to make everyone else happy. I love all of my 7 aunts and uncles, 50+ cousins and second cousins and great aunts and relatives that aren't really my relatives. They each make me feel greatly loved in one instant, with just a look. That is priceless.

Back to the Mayan calendar, a few months ago, I found some websites that discuss the Mayan calendar at length. I read it these days, almost daily, to help keep me in line with natural energies. I had a taste of so many wonderful and new things 7 years ago. It's time to dive into the things that suit me. I have returned to Philadelphia a much stronger and wiser woman than when I left and I have many experiences and adventures still to be explored.

That is the main reason I brought up the tarot deck. Last night, I consulted the cards for guidance on a personal matter. One of my cards was "The World" card. It shows a snake in a circle biting its tail with a hermaphrodite in the middle. The card means that as one journey ends, at the same time, another begins. There is no breaking of the cycle. The one constant is change. I knew this card well! The hermaphrodite represents masculine and feminine energy in one (yin/yang). It is the combination of the two energies that keeps the one wheel of life turning. The opposing forces create movement. They don't have to clash. It can be harmonious, balanced and powerful.

Just as human beings too, shed our layers of skin, this book marks the ending of an "era" in my life and the beginning of a new one.

I've seen this reflected in many of my journals. I've ended countless books at the same time major things in my life were ending- or beginning. Where DOES one end and another begin, aside from the various labels "we" put on "them"? The largest organ of our body is what many see as some sort of shield, our skin. It's an organ, not a great divide. For the sake of ease in "normal" communication, I'm going to label these pages as my book and allow you the choice to see these words as the end or the beginning.

Life is challenging enough in some way or another, for us all. "Follow your bliss." might seem too trite to some to help carry on and FULLY live another moment, but whatever it takes to summon that sense of/connection with spirit from the core of your being-
for all of us (please) do so.

It
IS
essential
and invisible.
It can not be sold or bought,
but
IT
does
LIVE
and breathes-
within
us ALL,
Here-
for us,
by us,
with us.

It
IS
Us.
My Love,
Life.
Now, let's give us a GREAT, BIG, WARM hug....
and continue on....
Shall we?

Let us….

In Love,

For Love,

Feel Love,

Be Love,

With Love,

My Love,

From Love.

*The following was written within 5-10 minutes during my week of recording. I sampled one of my songs' hooks and wrote this off the top of my head. It was eye opening for me on many levels.

"What would u choose?"

I bear the pains, yeah.
I see its stains.
I also taste its sweet, yesss,
It makes me so weak...

When I feel that pulse,
I cannot help but to cry
It's more than worth it though
To enjoy the letting go.

'Cause you're deep inside
In my mind
In my heart
In my soul
Never growing old.

You haven't missed a day,
But I've been away
Never thought I'd stay
I curse the day

I let go of your hand,
Thought I was rather grand.
Didn't overstand
And here I am

Back here with you,
My boo,
Through and through...
For me and for you.

It's here to share
If you care,
Or rather, dare,
To be somewhere

Preferrably,
You can see
Abundantly,
For eternity.

Why not here?
Why not now?
How's that sound?
Give it a round.

See how it goes.
Who knows?
Just maybe,
You will be...

Astonished and bemused
Or thoroughly confused.

What would you do?

What would you choose?

* I decided to include the following seven poems as "bonus material" to be read, digested and reread for insight and pleasure for ages to come. Hopefully, it will prevent this book from simply collecting dust wherever it may be.

TO MY FELLOW HUMANS

O people, my people,
O sky, my sky
Magnificent and so shy
Gentle and meek
Upon my cheek
Kissing the sun
My beloved One
O park, my park
O moon, my moon!
So far away
And here I stay
To dream of lives
Beyond the skies
Created anew
As the morning dew.
My head rests at last
The wrongs of my past
Are now wiped clean-
Here is what I mean...
O human, my Human
O people, my People
In this wondrous world of ours
At our core we are all equal.

(written in Washington Square Park in 2000)

WO/MAN, BE NOT ASHAMED OR AFRAID

Feeling cheesy and rather romantic
At times it's just the hopeless part...
That's when climes are really dark.
Changing hormones keep their pace
A relaxed and focused mind wins the race.
Lashing in spite doesn't help an ounce
Though at times there's pleasure in the pounce.
Two steps back for every one gained
What's It worth during trials and pains?
Finding strength
From no where in sight-
A Life lesson meant
To give us might.
Building and growing
Planting and sowing
Exploring and knowing
Ebbing and Flowing
Nature, now and all ways,
Comforts with the sun's rays
Even in night's thickest haze
No matter how complex the maze.
True love's a bond uniting US ALL
Permeating even the THICKEST walls.
Every human can BE, here and NOW
Simply breathing deeply, FEEL and ALLOW.

I WAS THERE, REMEMBER?

I was there when you leaned over and kissed me.
I was there....
I was there,
feeling your ear with my tongue,
listening to your breath
as you gasped for air.
I heard your words of astonishment.
I felt the luxurous warmth of our embrace.
I feel it now.
My world is replete; filled with these sensations.
Wholeness. Completion.
There is no wanting,
Only satisfaction.
We could do no wrong.
We can do no wrong.
So succint...
I'm still there,
Right here.
You have my undivided attention.
Exploring new heights,
Surpassing my greatest expectations.
Whatever you ask of me,
I do.
Love's slave.
Love's master.
In each other
We are worshipped
And glorified.
Why do I believe all of these things?
Because I was there,
Remember?

ECSTACY'S WAKE

I've no clue what I'm going to do next.
No idea.
But no matter what, I'll love you
And I'll feel WONDERFUL doing it!
I'll love you beyond my wildest dreams.
I already do
And will continue to.
Stay as long as you like.
Leave as long as you wish.
We are always together
United
by the the bonds of love.
You are forever with me
And me with you,
Bringing out the best in everything we do.
My soul,
My body,
My mind,
My heart
CRIES OUT
In the
Uni-verse....
And I take a deep breath....
And listen to it's beautiful echo....
Basking in Ecstacy's wake.

A VOICE

I've heard her standing beside me
Making me feel as though I am a prize.
She believes in me so vehemently
and helps me see many truths from lies.
I tingled in her presence.
Her beauty was simple and pure.
Her heart pours out sincerity.
With her, all trials I endure.
This being is my invisible best friend
With me through sadness and joy.
She only sees the star in me
The part we can never destroy.
I still hear her voice so clear
Sharing news of things to come.
The excitement and pleasure with which she speaks
Assures me it can and will be done.

TOUCHES

Music
TOUCHES
Me
all over...
All ways in my heart,
on my mind,
spending time
thinking of rhymes.

Living each day as a honey moon
is a great way to heal all wounds.
exploring past what is known,
why delay or postpone?

Many muses lie all about
Depending on your "reasonable" doubt
Perhaps if you're willing to check it out
You'll see why I have this urge to shout.

The beauty of life can be felt in a stare,
A moment, a glare without any care,
can inspire a prayer-
kind words passed through air.

Our thoughts do not cease
To offer some release.
Negativity does decrease,
This is the start of peace.

Take as much as you would like
Bask to your sheer delight
Do not worry about your plight
I am here each day and ev'ry night.

MAKING LOVE

How do I love thee, let me count the ways
Until the final moments of my days.
Seeking no thing I give you my all.
Not hiding behind a self-imposed wall.

A treasure beyond measure…

I let go-
so that I can hold on,
following my heart.
It's a very good place for me to start
Playing my part,
Making Love
The Ultimate
Art.

Love ALL ways

www.ingramcontent.com/pod-product-compliance
Lightning Source LLC
Chambersburg PA
CBHW031959040426
42448CB00006B/415